JOBA ADEKANMI

IT SEEMS THAT WITHOUT GOD, MAN CANNOT
AND WITHOUT MAN, GOD WILL NOT.
— JOHN WESLEY

RECOVER
Finding Help in times of need

Recover

ISBN 978-1-914528-05-7

Published in United Kingdom by:
Impact Publishing House

www.TheServantandKing.com
iph@TheServantandKing.com

CONTENTS

Contents

Introduction

Are you tired and frustrated because things are not just working out? Is your future looking bleak with no help in sight? Have you been overwhelmed with life and feel you cannot carry on any longer? Have you lost all, and you think it is all over? Do you require something essential to life, and it seems it is not going to happen? Are you on the verge of giving up? Whatever your situation may be, there is hope as long as you are still alive.

Everyone living has a need. Some seem to have more than others, or they can get most of what they require when they need it. Every human desires to have all their needs met, especially when they are essential to survival. It is not always so, unfortunately. Many people never get to that point; they never live to see that place they have so desired to be. They have more needs than they could comfortably handle.

What do you do when you have needs, and you have tried continuously to get them sorted, but it has never worked? Is there help anywhere? How do we get the help and support in our time of need?

Many people around the world have benefited from opportunities to get help. Many have suffered in silence because they could not access the essential assistance to keep them alive and productive. Many have died because they never realised that there was help for their situation. Some others could not imagine a solution was possible or available anywhere.

The answer you need may be closer than you could ever have imagined. In some cases, what could save the situation might be something simple. It could be a small change, but if not known, it could result in a tragedy.

A tourist may be at risk in the water if he does not know how to swim, but if you can call on the lifeguard in time, you could save a life that is about to drown in the water. If a patient can reach the hospital in time, the doctor may resuscitate the patient.

The help may be there, but it is also vital to know where it is and have the required access. A doctor can help with health problems, a fireman with fire problems. A lawyer can help sort out legal issues, and a teacher could assist with educational needs. They assist others but have needs as well that their expertise cannot handle. They also need to look for help concerning other areas of their lives.

How can we get the help we need to keep us going in life? How do we decide which assistance is best for us? How do we choose out of numerous options? How do we ascertain that it will meet our needs and not endanger our life or future?

It is like many things we do in our everyday life. It is possible to make a wrong decision which could lead to unpleasant consequences. It is the reason for so many undesired changes that have occurred to many people around the world.

The help we do or do not get in the time of need can go a long way in determining how far we can continue our lives or fulfil our goals. Two individuals may face almost the same challenges, but if they approach it differently, one may become better for it while the other may end up in a worse position. It is usually the case, especially when the necessary help to carry on was missing in the life of one of them. Many people are a function of the support they have received. You may find out that you could do better in life only if you harness the help that you need.

In this book, you will find some clear and actionable advice that will help to restore hope and encourage you to step out and make the most of any situation. It will help you in your journey to navigate your present or future challenges to fulfil your potential.

Chapter 1

IT IS NOT BIZARRE

Do you have needs that made you think of the worst? Have you ever thought you are in the strangest situation out of all the people living on earth? You are not alone. So many people find themselves in challenging situations from time to time, and some have been able to weather the storm. They came out the other end triumphant, but it is not always the case for everyone.

It is sometimes worrying to see what some people do when they have a need. They lose hope or give up, and some result in suicide. So many things could have led to such actions and decisions, but could this be avoided? Can this tragedy be turned around? It may be comforting for them to know that they are probably in a situation similar to or better off than someone else. It could also be helpful to understand that there could be a way out. Someone may have been in the same position at some point in time.

It is common to see people call the ambulance when there is an injury or drive the patient to the hospital. For example, if a child gets seriously injured on the playground, the parents will be worried and probably frightened. They will take the child to the hospital. Have you ever wondered why the medical team are usually not as terrified? They, experienced in treating such injuries, will not be as scared because they have seen such before—they know what to do to meet that need. They then try to pass on that confidence to the patient and hope to the parents, showing the way back to recovery.

One interesting thing you might also find in the hospital is that there are even worse cases—some that can make yours trivial. They are also likely to tell you if you inquire that so many other people have had the same experience.

It is similar in life. What you are going through is not strange. Your frustration could be because you do not know what to do.

It may be reassuring to know that what you are going through is what someone else has gone through, and someone in the future will still have to go through the same experience. It is not just you, so do not give up.

It might be different for different people, and some may know what to do while others may not know, some others may not even know that the help they require is possible.

Whatever has happened to you has almost certainly been experienced by someone before. It is always vital to know what to do. I found this to be true regardless of status, culture or nation.

Some may think they have needs because they are not in a particular profession or like certain people. They hope that their needs will disappear if they can swap positions. I wish they could ask those people; they will find out, they also have their own needs. The rich may not need money, but they also have necessities that make them seek help. There are needs everywhere, whether in London, New York, Paris or Sydney. Anywhere in the world. Individuals, families, communities, and nations all have needs. They all try to find a way to get their needs met. You do not have to see yourself as strange but seek the help you need.

The weak need help, the strong also need help. Do not commit suicide because of your needs. Seek help on what to do to get out of it.

While the needs of everyone may be different, the principle is the same. You can get out of that situation if you know what to do. The doctor needs something that his medical expertise cannot deliver. The teacher requires something that his skills cannot provide. The lawyer seeks help for a challenge that his legal skills cannot solve. The celebrities have needs that fame cannot meet. Everyone has to look for what they do not have.

It is normal to seek help. The wise understand this and take advantage of it. Why think of suicide because you failed an exam? It is not your end; get yourself together and get help. Whatever the situation you may find yourself in, there is hope for you. The appropriate assistance is all you need to get yourself back again.

You do not have enough money, and you want to kill yourself? It could be a difficult situation, but there is hope for you. All you require is to get access to the help you need. It may not be as bad as you think when you locate the support you require.

Are you thinking of ending your life? Is it because of loss? Did you lose your job as a cleaner, actor, lawyer, or director or in any other role? Take it easy. It is not strange. Managers lose their jobs. Ministers and Ambassadors lose their jobs, MPs wake up to discover that they no longer have a job. Governors lose their positions in elections. Presidents are voted out and have to come to terms with the reality. It is not strange. Do not commit suicide but seek help on what to do next. It is not the end. You can get help for the subsequent line of action—it is the wise thing to do.

Companies seek help—so they do not go into administration. Virgin Atlantic, among others, was seeking help to keep the company afloat during the pandemic. The business magnate and investor, Richard Branson, who founded the group, is a billionaire with influence, but they also seek help in need to keep them going.[1,2]

Communities are asking for help. Governments around the world are doing the same. They seek help for their needs. It is not bizarre, and it is not just you. If you cannot handle it anymore, cry out for help—it is wise.

It is not strange to have needs, so you do not have to think of doing anything disastrous in the time of need. Do not give up, but get help. *C'est ne pas bizarre, c'est normal.*

Chapter 2

THE EARLIER, THE BETTER

Do you have needs that have grown worse with time? Have you ignored your needs and discovered that they now constitute a threat to your life? Have you ever had a need but sought help too late?

It is often true that when you solve a problem early, it is likely to cost less and reduces the chances of getting worse. Early help may save the situation. There are times we lose the opportunity for recovery when we delay.

There are so many reasons for such hesitation, some of which are as follows: trivialising the issue, a false feeling that things are under control, indifferent attitude, ignorance, misplaced priority, fear, lack of resources, among others. It is crucial to seek help on time. You have a higher chance of remedy than waiting till later. The later you leave it, the more dangerous the situation and the more challenging the solution.

An employee that is receiving frequent warnings for poor performance should not ignore them. It will become worse if no action follows and eventually may lead to the loss of the job. Seeking early assistance may help to improve the performance of the individual in the same role. If that is not feasible, a better solution that could bring fulfilment as soon as possible would be a good idea.

Many people see signs of danger ahead in their organisation. It could be the signs of redundancy after the loss of a significant customer, policy changes, changes in government, competition and so on. They could be pointers to the fact that something is about to happen. It may not occur in some cases, but seeking help on time gives time to prepare ahead and avoid sudden disaster.

Imagine employees that spend more money than they earn. It could be a warning light that there is a problem. They might be able to return to a good position with good and early financial counsel. They may also choose to ignore the warning signs and continue borrowing. It may lead to more hardship. They may be accumulating debts that they may never be able to pay. A small loan with a high-interest rate may provide temporary relief but could lead to unpleasant situations in future with debts that they cannot pay off. Many have become bankrupt doing something similar.

A student may be struggling with tests and assessments. That is the best time to get help. The situation may be redeemable. The signs, if ignored, hoping everything will be fine, may make things worse. He may fail to attain the required grades to progress, leading to a withdrawal or dismissal. It becomes more complicated and more stressful.

A toe injury may look small and may not seem dangerous. If not treated properly could lead to infections, in worse cases, the amputation of the foot. The problem can get worse if not treated on time. The help needed increases as the conditions get worse. A first aider or a nurse may be the help required within a short period of the incident. The more time spent doing nothing may cause more harm. It may become critical, in which case, it may require the help of a doctor or a Specialist if it has gone worse. When the foot becomes infected, the only solution would be to amputate the leg, in some cases. The patient has benefited from lots of assistance, but the loss is more. Less received on time could indeed have retained more value. The earlier, the better.

It is like driving a car with signs of a faulty braking system. The driver could decide to seek help as soon as possible. A mechanic is all that is needed to resolve the problem. If ignored or postponed, the signs and condition will get worse. It is an accident going somewhere to happen. It is a question of when not if. The more time that elapses without seeking help, the more the risks of injury and damage. It could lead to an accident affecting other people as well. The assistance required is now more, probably specialist doctors for the people involved, but if there is a fatality, then it becomes too costly. The car will always need more help for repairs which would be more expensive than the cost of the initial problem. It is always better sooner than later.

There are a lot of people suffering from the effect of delayed responses to their needs in life.

The initial problem has increased to become so challenging and complicated because it has expanded over time without seeking help. It now looks like an irredeemable situation. You may need more help, but it may probably be a recoverable situation. There is still hope if you have found yourself in such circumstances. You need to act now without further delay.

THE MORE TIME THAT ELAPSES WITHOUT SEEKING HELP, THE MORE THE RISKS OF INJURY AND DAMAGE.

Chapter 3

RECOGNISE YOUR NEED

There are so many questions that come our way in the course of our day. Some are easier to answer than others. Some make us happy, while some could make us sad. One could be the question we have been waiting for, while another could be the one that we would rather have loved to avoid. Have you ever required help, and you got an offer for assistance? I wonder what your response was or would be.

Many people have opportunities for assistance, but they are lost because they do not know what they need. Help is available most often than not, but many do not understand what they need.

They lose the opportunity because they think they need something else.

Imagine a young boy that says he needs money. You then ask him how much and the purpose. He responds by saying the amount and that he would like to buy the latest iPhone. Why an iPhone? you inquire. 'I need an iPhone to call home in case of emergency when I am in school.' He stated his need—money, but you can probably deduce something different from his response. He also suggested an iPhone, but his answer provides another requirement. It seems that all he requires is a suitable device 'to call home in case of emergency when I am in school.' His need was in his response but appeared after the word iPhone—which he thought was his need.

If you consider the young man and his need, you may find many possible ways to meet that need without buying an iPhone. It seems a means of communication is all that is required. So many people may be able to help this young man with his request, but he may not get help because he presented it as something different.

Many people may not give him sufficient money to buy an iPhone, and they may not donate the latest iPhone either. However, It is more likely that several people can help with solving his communication problem. Communication is the need is here; there are many different ways to achieve it without any of those things he stated. It could be through another brand of phone, a used phone that someone is willing to give away, probably access to other communication devices, or any other means available to those that could be of help.

It is a graphic picture of the situation of so many people today. They ask for what they do not need and those that can help turn away. They have what you need but not what you are requesting. There are so many times where people ask for help but lose out because they ask for the wrong thing. If you require assistance, your responses may determine whether or not people can assist you.

It is common to find that some people only ask for money. It may be true that you can always buy what you want when you have money, but countless other things could meet the same need. A hungry man can get food or a voucher to use in any restaurant of choice instead of money. A lady struggling to pay her rent may have many offers for assistance that could be beneficial. It could include a house with lower rent and fewer expenses. A man struggling to pay his bills may get some support options that could assist with getting a better job or a recruiter. Several people can contribute their quota without giving cash directly to them.

You may have ignored people that could help you because they did not give you what you expected. It is vital to understand what you require, and that will help you get help quicker. Have you tabled your request before a potential helper, and you got the unexpected and unfavourable reply; 'Sorry I cannot help you.' They may be able to help you, but most often than not, it represents an answer that implies 'You do not know what you need.'

There is so much help that you can get from others that will not necessarily involve the exchange of money. You could benefit from skills, services, assets, counsel, connections, experience, comfort, time, presence, exposure and recommendations of others. They could be worth much more than money, but only a few people value it, yet fewer take advantage of it.

A mother was once frustrated with her daughter as she throws tantrums uncontrollably, refusing all kinds of food. She got worried because her daughter was losing weight, growing thinner, would not engage or interact anymore. She had the money to buy her anything she wanted, but that did not solve the problem. The simple solution came when she met with another family with a daughter of similar age. It was like she found her long lost joy. The daughter was eating, playing and having fun even with less expensive toys—cheaper than those bought by her parents or that they could afford. I wonder how one would value that experience in terms of money. It was priceless for this mother and liberating for her daughter. They found the right help for their need.

Several people struggle to get one thing while there is help to meet their actual needs close to them. They ignored it because it does not look like what they have in mind. It is like a battle for shadows while neglecting the real thing. You may need to reconsider what you are longing to get so that you can make progress. There may be help hovering around you, but you never realised it was all you need.

THERE IS SO MUCH HELP THAT YOU CAN GET FROM OTHERS THAT WILL NOT NECESSARILY INVOLVE THE EXCHANGE OF MONEY.

Chapter 4

SEARCH FOR HELP

The needs of human beings are diverse, and the solutions required by each one can be variant. It is challenging for some, probably confusing and daunting for others. There are probably a few that do not even have any clue. Have you found yourself in such a position of need? Have you considered all your various and complex needs and only become more frustrated and confused? Have you tried, but it is not getting any better, but it has become worse? Many may be able to relate to this position. A lot of people have been there. What do you do when you are in need and do not know what to do?

The challenges of life could be overwhelming. It may be easier for some than others. There are times you could be in a situation you have never witnessed before, where you have no idea of what to do, neither do you know where to turn. What do you do?

It may be new to you, but it may not be the same for everyone else as they may have some information or experience that you lack. Almost eight billion people are living in the world today, across races, cultures, and nationalities. The world is full of people like you and me. They face similar life challenges and experiences. It may not always be the same, but it is not uncommon either. Some of the things you are going through must have happened to someone living or who has lived.

Most often than not, many look for answers only in their comfort zone. They seek assistance only from those that look like them. They explore only the familiar things and believe anything from that source without verification. It may have been a good idea with reasons and probably a safe strategy for some people, but it has become, for some others, the end of their search and termination of their hope. They lost hope in finding help and made permanent resolutions because of their temporary circumstances.

It is one thing to recognise your need, but it is another to know where and how to get the help you need. Every question has an answer; every problem has a solution. You may not know the answer, but that does not mean there is none. The truth is that you do not yet know and probably do not know who knows. There are answers and solutions, but you need to search for them till you find what you need.

It is a burden to search for answers or solutions. Many people have done so with a significant part of their lives. The world is privileged to have such rich resources which are available for the benefit of all. Today, it would be fair to say that it would be quicker to find such answers than it would have been many years ago. You may not need to search too long before you get what you need, but you still need to invest time in an issue-oriented search for answers.

The search for answers also comes with another problem. It is the ability to know whether what you have found is what you need and applicable to your circumstance. Many answers are available, but not all are true. You may discover that as far as your situation is concerned, they are not apposite. You not only need the answers but one that is right for you.

Some people have allergic reactions to nuts, for instance. It has been very severe in some cases. Some would never believe that the food they loved so much could be the reason for their tragedy. They thought it would be everything else but that 'good thing' they love to eat. Some found help, and they got relevant information on what to do to overcome it, and some others avoided it when they understood it was the reason for their reactions. You can see two different approaches to the same problem. It depends on where you turn for help.

I have come across some people that have prolonged health issues. They have attempted all medical advice and tried everything that comes to their mind, but all to no avail. A search for answers revealed it was the presence of gluten in their diet. It was liberating, but it was not one of those things they would have thought of, but unfortunately, that is the cause of the problem. Sadly, many others have the same problem, still suffering under the same conditions until they hopefully stumble on the solution. They may continue in frustration as they seek help in the wrong places and make uninformed decisions.

Some time ago, I was excited to observe changes in one of our local stores—it was a whole aisle stocked up with only gluten-free products. It is the answer to some peoples questions, the help to someone's need. There are so many people suffering from the challenges of life that they do not understand, and those around them also cannot figure it out. It is like allergies which require relevant knowledge to figure out. If you do not understand or know what to do, it could be disastrous. You will get more frustration going to the wrong places or attempting the problem with your limited knowledge.

An American psychologist, Abraham Maslow once said; 'If the only tool you have is a hammer, you tend to see every problem as a nail.' You may have found this to be true. Trying to solve every problem the same way is the simple reason for the frustration of many. You need to search for help that takes into account the uniqueness or peculiarity of the situation. If you go to the wrong person, you will get the wrong counsel. It may have worked for him but could be bad for you.

Everyone is searching for help for different challenges. It is not just the help that counts, but one that matches their peculiar need.

An expert mechanic that offers to help with brain damage may put you in danger. A pilot that offers to help a farmer with an infestation may cause more harm than good. A nurse trying to advise on legal issues may put you in trouble. A chef willing to help in a medical surgery to correct a physical deformity is likely to magnify the pain. They are all experts in their field but may not have enough expertise or experience to help you in meeting your need. It is a good idea to learn to discern and to choose what is best for you.

Your needs may be different, and as such, you may have tried all you know, and there seems to be no hope. Do not die in silence. Do not give up yet; search, do some research, explore, gather facts and make sound and informed decisions based on your discovery. Help may be closer than you ever imagined.

Chapter 5

WOLVES IN SHEEP'S CLOTHING

Many times we get the assistance that gives us temporary relief and a sense of progress. It becomes a different experience after a while when we discover that it did not help after all. Have you been there? Have you found yourself receiving assistance but later found that it did more harm than good? You may have figured out that your assessment was not accurate. You probably thought they were for you, but it turns out that they were against you or your goal.

The search for help could be a challenging one. Answers may not always come as fast or easy as expected, but sometimes, surprises seem to beat our expectations and cause us to react spontaneously. We go all out for it and ignore every other important detail. Have you received help and wondered why? Have you gotten a gift and felt; what is the motive behind this? Have you considered why some people want to help you and not someone else? You will find some interesting answers as you ask questions and study those involved.

People help for many reasons, but it may be hard to understand the motive behind their actions sometimes. It could be a good opportunity, but it could also be a trap. Help can come from well-meaning people and those with intentions that you are not aware of or one that is not known. It could sometimes be to your disadvantage or your hurt. They could present themselves as calm and unharmful like sheep, but they could be dangerous wolves. It is vital to focus not only on your need but also on the source of help. Do not grab every offer blindly; find out more, understand the reasons behind it, and make informed decisions. It could be a trap that could rob you in the future.

Some people have had unpleasant experiences because of desperation. They accept anything that comes without careful consideration and later found themselves in bondage. A sweet beginning of help left a bitter or sour taste afterwards. There are so many things in life that are not as they seem.

A time of need is often a time of frustration, anxiety or fear, and many take advantage of this position to exploit. Many people offer services to exploit the vulnerability of others. There are so many companies that offer to dispose of cars, some equipment, or a house, for instance. They give you false hope just for you to buy their services, and as soon as they get you, their attitude changes—you discover they are not really who you think they were. They aim to make their gain, not for you to get the help you need. Many have been frustrated because they sought help. They desired it but ended in a worse situation.

A young man once sought help after a motor accident that rendered his car a write-off. He promptly got an offer for a brand new replacement car which he gladly accepted. He signed all the documents and began to enjoy his new automobile. The service was quick, and the delivery of the car was like the speed of light. The impression he had was that the bill was nothing for him to worry about, but he was wrong. A few weeks afterwards, he got a call to return the car or pay more charges—he had to pay the bill to his surprise. The insurance company did not pay because he did not qualify for it. It all went pear-shaped because of some small print in the agreement brought to his attention afterwards. The comfort did not last long. He was perplexed when he saw the bill that amounts to thousands of pounds. The story could have been different if he considered the offer well and checked the details.

Some nations have found themselves in a worse position because of the support they received. They were excited to get the funds that were not in the best interest of the nation. The assistance has taken more from them than it has added to them. It led them backwards and not forward.

For some others, it could be a job offer or a juicy appointment in exchange for immoral acts or favours. If it does not look right, it is a red flag. If you are not eligible for such, it may be a trap. Whenever you notice that there is a selfish gain, they are not interested in helping you. They are only doing all to achieve their selfish aim.

Some lecturers use their students to satisfy their lustful desires. They present themselves as supportive, willing to assist struggling students, but their main aim is what they want to gain. They have left many with emotional trauma and frustrations. It is frustrating and demoralising to be robbed by those that should protect and help.

Some leaders take advantage of the vulnerability of their followers. They rob instead of supporting them. Many with similar attitudes have mastered the act so much that many are not aware of the wrongs. The victims continue to suffer the pain and agony for a long time. It is crucial to exercise caution—even when in need—so that you do not end up in bondage disguised as help.

There are so many things to watch out for in such people, among which is deceit. If you can sense it, it is a sign that danger is ahead. It will be in your good interest to avoid such.

Consistency is another one to look out for in people. If you observe that the helper keeps changing, negating former promises, or their words do not match the actions, it may be someone to avoid. It is better to wait longer than to get help in a hurry and end up in trouble.

Many have become victims of fraudsters in a bid to seek a better life in a different country. It has been an unpleasant experience for some and a death trap for many others. Many people have lost the little they had to some seemingly good people who deceived them. They only make ridiculous promises—they could never deliver, to deceive, not to fulfil it.

You may have needs and many seemingly good options, but some of them may be traps in disguise. Be calm and check well before you make your decisions. You do not have to destroy your future because of the help you received today. Your needs may have put you in a challenging situation, but it is crucial to be cautious; so that you do not make it worse. Do not be in a hurry. Please take your time to consider every case properly; you may be dealing with a wolf in the clothing of a sheep.

Chapter 6

HELP IS NEAR, I NEVER KNEW

We all face challenging and difficult times in life. Most often than not, many have a preconceived idea of where they expect help. It may be a good and effective strategy, but sometimes it has robbed some of the opportunity to ask for assistance outside of those conventional ways.

Have you been in a situation where you were expecting assistance from someone far away or in a particular way, which you imagined should work, but got frustrated after many trials?

Some have discovered afterwards that help was closer than they imagined. Many times we ignore those around us while they have in their hands the answers we need. We often only appreciate what is farther away. Some others may even accept that help is not available anywhere.

We have help all around us, but sometimes we cannot recognise it. Some people have the answers to their questions as close to them as possible, like families, friends, colleagues, or neighbours. Some ignore these close people and go all out for help, but never realise that the person living in the same house with them has the answer. It may not always be the case, may not always be the same for everybody, or every circumstance. Some people would find that it could be significant and lifesaving.

Some people know what you do not yet know, and they are around you, probably in your family. It is help available for you as close as it can be. It may be anything from explanation or guidance for schoolwork to advice on life choices, counsel on handling difficult, challenging or unfamiliar life situations. They may not have all you need, but the initial help they provide could be priceless. There will always be something in life that is happening to you for the first time. It is also true that some people around you have gone through that experience—they could help you through it.

Many young boys and girls often ignore wise counsel and trust more in themselves or their peers. They accept information that comes from sources that do not have their best interest at heart. Many young people have made critical mistakes because of this and have become a victim of evil. It may not be impossible that some people have had a very horrible experience from those around them. They might have come to a different conclusion as far as they are concerned, but help could be closer than we think. There are people around you that have your best interest at heart, and their counsel could go a long way in getting your feet on the right path.

I once listened to a brain-function specialist, Arlene R. Taylor, talk about the brain and its development. It was interesting to know that some parts of the brain become fully mature at about twenty-seven. The frontal cortex matures last, even though every other part of the brain is present and developed. The region houses the executive functions, and they help with some skills including, planning, self-monitoring, time management, self-discipline, organisation, and thinking.[1] It explains why so many young people make wrong long life decisions, as they may not have the capacity to understand the implications. It could be responsible for the unexpected behaviours we see around us because they attempt to make lifelong decisions before their brain matures. Some people are behind bars for criminal offences and could not understand the implications. It is possible to stop this pattern by seeking guidance from those that have gone ahead, especially for decisions that have a lifelong impact. There could be some people around you, closer than you could ever think that could help.

My family once lived next door to a young man. He was struggling and frustrated. He was into drugs and had a different lady almost every week to stay with him. There were always arguments, fighting, throwing furniture at each other, among other things. It was challenging to have a quiet night. He was a troubled young man looking for a solution but did not know the way out. Eventually, he found help next door. He saw the possibility to live differently without doing the things he was doing. I was glad to help, and he was willing to receive it. He decided against drugs and chose to start a new course in life. He was eventually free from the addiction, married a professional lawyer, and continued on the same path.

Do you have needs and do not understand what to do? Have you concluded that no one can help? Have you begun a journey to self-destruction? Stop and think. There may be help around you that you probably have ignored or never appreciated. Many people have gone through the same experience, and their counsel could be the help you need. Be humble and accept it. It may be closer to you, but that does not reduce the value. Most of the things we do not appreciate in life tend to be the most significant things.

It would be a good idea to take your time to carefully consider all you have around you, ensuring you choose a trusted and reliable source for help. You may discover that all you have been waiting for is by your side but never knew it.

WE HAVE HELP ALL AROUND US, BUT SOMETIMES WE CANNOT RECOGNISE IT.

Chapter 7

How Did I Get here?

There are so many decisions we make in life. Some produce the change we anticipate, while others lead us to unexpected ends. Sometimes, we have problems because of a decision or choice we have made. One that did not go quite well or that threw us out of our control.

Have you sincerely asked yourself the question: 'How did I get here?' 'How did I find myself in this situation?' The answers could be the help you need.

You may be facing challenging times, you need help, but it seems it is not forthcoming. An assessment of your life and decisions may help in the journey back to recovery. So many things could have contributed to the position you find yourself in, but some self-assessment questions will go a long way in providing clarity. You are likely to get help or be directed aright if you know what you need.

A student that refuses to attend classes or complete assignments may eventually face dismissal. He can enrol in a different school as a quick fix, but that may not bring the desired change if the same attitude continues. A critical look into the situation will reveal the need that produced the unpleasant result. There are so many times in life that we ignore the cause and try to fix the effects. Nothing happens suddenly, and if we can identify the reason, we are in a better position to get the relevant help.

An employee with a recent poor performance could come across as unserious, lazy or unintelligent. The effect is visible, but what is the cause? Why is she unable to do what she ought to do? A closer look into the situation will reveal more details. She may have been going through some personal issues or challenging circumstances lately, affecting her ability or state of mind. It could be some environmental factors that are making her uncomfortable. She may be affected by harassment or bullying. It may be fear or threats. The effects are visible, but most often than not, there is no consideration for the possible causes with the view of getting help.

Some children struggle to learn in school. They find it difficult to express their ability. They are so unique that those around them do not know what they need. They do well in so many other things in life but struggle in academics. It could be a burden to thrive under conventional learning methods. A change of environment or approach could be the help they need.

A lot of people copy others to follow a particular lifestyle or choice of career. They soon begin to struggle and discover that fulfilment is far away, and challenges stare them in the face. An evaluation of their decisions may reveal where they have gone wrong. It is common to see people go into business or a particular career for the profit, glamour, fame, honour or convenience that comes with it. The more they progress, the more miserable and frustrated they become.

They did not consider the losses, hard work, self-denial and risks that a successful Businessman or woman would have to bear. They only think of the holidays, cars, and yachts that come at the end. They wanted to be great, but they found that it was not as easy as they thought, so they get crushed by the unforeseen challenges that came their way.

It is a misconception that has made many people worse off. Some have invested their life savings in a venture that they have no idea of how it works, hoping to make millions in a short period. Some sell their belongings to get rich quickly. Many have ended up in debt, and some even turned beggars as a result. It is better to treat the cause than to manipulate the effects.

You may have found that some people are a victim of influence. They follow a lifestyle that they cannot sustain with their income and eventually become needy. They keep struggling to keep up but never tell themselves the truth nor discover the cause of their predicament. Some people do not like to be themselves as they always desire to be like someone else. They never see the importance of their uniqueness. They keep living without satisfaction because they want to be someone else, not themselves. They live all their life to please some other people but displease themselves. The help they need is to learn to appreciate their uniqueness and not to become like someone else.

A breadwinner that gambles with the family finances hoping to get billions of pounds in return; may lose everything, putting the whole family in need. If income increases or they get financial assistance, gambling is likely to increase. The problem then gets worse and not better. The cause is the idea of gambling—giving something of value for an uncertain outcome. They have money but do not manage it well. They voluntarily take the money to the casino, only to return home with no food or drink. It is the story of many families around the world. Help that focuses on the cause rather than the effects will produce an effective result.

Do you know the reason for your needs? That is what you need help with, do not ignore the cause and dance around the effects. If you do not treat the problem, you will soon find yourself in the same position of need. We often see some people attempt to change the effects but not digging deep into the causes.

An employee was living fine after so many years of working. He got promoted at work, his taste changed to match a particular status. It was not long afterwards that he had debt problems with threats from debtors. Something must have has gone wrong. An assessment of how he spends his money will reveal the situation. He probably made a significant change to his spending pattern that he could not sustain. He needs help to detect that and get back on track.

You might have heard of stories of people that decided to makes changes in their life. It could be in their career, lifestyle, approach, environment, or influence. They probably discovered themselves and found that they are in the wrong place or made choices for the wrong reasons. You may need to revisit your decisions and make the relevant changes.

Are you dissatisfied with where you are? Are you disappointed? Are you in need and desire help? You are not alone. You may have found yourself in the wrong place, struggling to make sense of your situation. There is help for you. Please, take time to consider your decisions and how you got to where you are. It may be the revelation you require to find the help you need.

Chapter 8

CHANGE BEGINS WITH YOU

The challenges of life have made many people find themselves in a position they never desired. Some may not be as bad as others, or probably the effects may have varying impacts. Many things go through the mind at those times, as there is a desire for change or help. What do you do at such times? What is the first thing that comes to your mind?

Sometimes, some people think that help can only come from everyone else except themselves. They continue to wait for other people to do something about the situation while they could do something to change their circumstances. You may not have everything you need, but you can start with yourself. You may be the help you need to get started.

Have you found the reason for being where you are? You can begin by starting a process of change by making the necessary corrections. You may have followed a particular lifestyle that has brought you shame and unfulfillment. You can begin a continuous step to change your lifestyle.

You may have discovered after an assessment that your losses were because of insufficient knowledge or skill. You can work on how to improve those areas. Should you need further help, you are informed enough to know where to turn, what to ask, as you have a specific area of focus. If you expect your situation to change, you must initiate the change. If you don't, it may remain the same or probably be affected by other changes by someone else which may not be in your interest.

If you lose your job because of redundancy, you may get another job in the relevant industry with your relevant skills. If you do not act, it may become harder the longer you stay jobless. If you do nothing still, you may begin to lose those skills. A time may come when you think of other industries or just anything to get money. It is like a gradual decline; in some cases, people may take advantage of that situation to offer you anything or use your skills or time for their selfish goals.

A student that knows that he failed because he did not study could correct that error by preparing well and sit the next exam. Most often than not, we can change our situation by sincerity to ourselves. You know the reason why you failed, then change, and you would get a better result. If you need help, get help in those areas you have identified. It is easier than blaming people, complaining or expecting that change will happen by doing nothing.

You may have attended a series of job interviews and never had success. You probably had some feedback about your performance. It could be at the interview or via correspondence. I hope you have not been throwing them away or ignoring the contents. It may contain some details that will help you. If you know why you were not selected, you could improve on those issues highlighted and apply for another job. You do not have to give up or get frustrated. You have the answer right before you, do the required, and soon you will be employed.

Have you thought of what you can do about your situation? You probably have been rejected for promotion because of poor performance. You will do well to request more details of the assessment. You can then find out what you can do to improve your performance and try again. The more information you have, the better the decisions you make.

You did not meet the requirement for a course for a reason. Find out how you can get the requirements and apply again. You may not always agree with what is required or the feedback provided, but at the least, you can get the relevant information to help make you a better person for your desired goal or future. Your situation will not change until you decide to change.

An investigation usually takes place after a major accident like a plane crash. The purpose, among other things, is to identify what went wrong to avoid recurrence. It could be related to anything or anyone, including the pilot, environment, engines, electronics, passengers, manufacturer, and so on. Information will be required to find the root cause of the matter. The investigation reveals the problem that now determines the appropriate action to follow. The airline will do all they can to avoid a reoccurrence because they will act on the discovered facts to fix the identified issues. They can then pass on with confidence the assurance they have through the discovery to the passengers. They will lose all their customers if they decide to do nothing.

Imagine you had a plan to manage a business for five years with the hope that you would make some profit. You found that after ten years of doing all you know to do, you incurred more losses than gain. Something must have gone wrong; you may not be as equipped as you thought, or many other things could be the result. You may need to find out and fix the issue.

I know some people that borrow money to start a business or investment. They hope to pay back the money within a short period of say six or twelve months. After the initial expiration period, they do not have the gain expected, let alone the capital. They now try to borrow some more, and their assurance is that they can pay off the former and latter debt with some gain in another twelve months of doing the same thing. They seem to think that the failure has nothing to do with them but just external forces that will work favourably with more borrowing at a different time. They often end up with more debts and frustration. I would have thought they would find out; Why did it not work the first time? What did I do wrong? The answer could help produce a better result.

Have you been copying some people, but you are not getting the anticipated result or unfulfilled? Something is not quite right. Find out where you missed it and initiate a change for good. You have the power to start that change whenever you are ready or tired of your situation.

You may have been hoping to win the lottery for the past 20 years. You were giving your last, but you have never won the hundreds of millions you desperately desired. What makes you think it would be any different if you continue in the same course for the next 30 years. If your chances of winning are 1 in 300,000,000 people, Is there hope? Can you put your life at a standstill because of such uncertainty? You may achieve more within a short period if you are willing to make the necessary change. It starts with you.

Some people make products, and no one shows interest—no sales. There is a reason; discover it, if you refuse to do so, you will soon be frustrated, wasting all your resources on items that would be thrown away or given out for free. You will do well to stop incurring losses, hoping that other people will change their minds. You may need to change.

The purpose of correction in a class is to help students identify their errors, correct them and progress in learning. If you are not progressing and refuse correction, it is like a decision to stay in the same position of need, yet you know what to do to experience a change.

Have you found out the reason for your present circumstance? Do you know what has gone wrong? Have you spotted your errors? That is help for you. Take the appropriate steps to make the change that is required. Change can happen at any time in life. You may realise that you have gone the wrong way; you can decide when to change. Do not let fear or the opinion of others keep you in bondage. Let the change start with you; let it be now.

YOUR SITUATION WILL NOT CHANGE
UNTIL YOU DECIDE TO CHANGE.

Chapter 9

THE DAY I CHOSE TO FLOURISH

Many years ago, I was a college student. My mother gave me some money, which was all that she could afford. I had to use it to meet all my needs till I could return home after the break. I collected the money with gratitude and departed for school. I was thinking of all the things I needed for school and how I could get them. There were many things, but the funds were limited.

I continued my journey and thought of getting one of the things on my list—toothpaste. I went to a store on my way to purchase the item. I asked for a particular brand called *Close-up*, by Unilever.

You may wonder why. It was because I was used to that brand. My parents bought it, it was popular, and by default, it was always the choice.

However, there was a problem, as I attempted to buy the toothpaste that I have always used. Do you know what the problem was? I realised that if I bought the toothpaste, I would not have enough money left—the cost was equal to a quarter of all I had on me.

It was a well-known product, and I have used it for many years. I could attest to its quality. There was a potential problem I saw at that time, considering my situation. If I bought it, I may not only have to clean my teeth with it, but probably have to eat it, drink it, and use it to meet my other needs. The decision to go for it could lead me to chaos.

I was standing in front of this product; I began to think. It occurred to me, after some considerations, that there was nothing on earth forcing me to buy the product except for the previous knowledge I had through my family. I thought further, 'What will happen to me if I do not purchase this product?' I thought of many things, one of which was that I would be deviating from what I had known, I will be departing from tradition. On the other hand, I would meet my needs and live without being frustrated, stranded or in debt. I could only choose one or the other.

I consciously moved my eyes away from the product to others in the same aisle, same shelf, some on the right, left, top and below. I was earlier considering the smallest size of *Close-up*, but I could not afford it. I looked at the other brands as well as their prices. One caught my attention, among many others. It was a bigger size, yet cheaper than the smallest size of *Close-up*. It means it could meet my need for longer. The product was called *Flourish* by PZ Cussons.

I was still trying to manage the change in my thoughts and process the implications to justify the shift. I read through the details and discovered that it was a viable replacement and affordable for me based on the budget I had at that time. It will do the job.

I then held the product in my hand as I concluded—I was happy to go ahead. I said to myself as I stood in the aisle: 'Why should I *Close-up* when it is in my power to *flourish?*' Why should I buy one thing that will cause me to be unable to function in other areas while I have the power to choose something else that I could afford, which could still do the same job?

There may be so many people in the same situation today. I am sharing this not to advertise or promote any company or product. It is not to justify any product, but to share my experience to help some people in the same circumstance. Many people hold onto traditions, which may not be a bad thing in itself. The problem arises when they can no longer afford it, and probably they do not realise. They never discern that it is the reason they do not have enough to meet other needs.

You probably had always bought luxurious or expensive products when you had a high paying role. You never realised the need to change when your income changed to a low paying one or fluctuating income. You may be choosing to *close-up* when you have the power to *flourish*, even in such a situation. You may be enjoying so many products and services when you are staying with your parents. You may need to change when you leave to be on your own. You may not be able to afford the same things. Operate at your level, so you do not get into difficulties. We all experience change, and change is for a season. It is not permanent. You must be willing to change to help you flourish in your temporary situation—otherwise, it may get worse.

Are you experiencing a change of circumstances? There could be a clue around you. There may be something you can change such that you can still flourish in the context of your new situation.

If you had always enjoyed lunch in an expensive restaurant, you probably want to consider other sources for balanced and healthy diets or try cooking for a change. It will go a long way to save you money. If you keep spending so much on food and do not have as much coming in as before, you will have more needs unmet. A conscious choice is required to make things better.

You may be used to buying only expensive designer clothes, but you will soon run into trouble if you keep up that tradition when you experience a change in your circumstance. It is either you let go of it or have your other needs unmet. It is in your power to make that decision.

Sometimes, you may discover that people do not pay for what they need. They pay to maintain social status. It is about pleasing other people that may not care. If you have a car that you can no longer afford to keep: would it not be better to let it go, get another one (if you cannot do without it) that you could afford, which could do the same job? Is it better to keep the luxurious car while your whole family cannot have a decent meal? You have the power to choose.

Some people have expensive entertainment subscriptions, which they are happy to keep or extend, and later beg for food. Many people renew contracts, take on upgrades or various additional devices and later complain that they do not have money. The reason for their need could be that they never realised that there are things they could change.

People struggle to meet their needs but do not realise that they could flourish if only they are willing to change. They think of the brand and not function or purpose. They look for what others are buying and not what will meet their own need.

Have you chosen a particular brand in the past to satisfy your preference or taste? Was your choice based on the expectation of others? Now that things have changed, probably temporarily, think of function and get a functional replacement that you can easily afford. You will do well and have peace of mind.

Look around you, considering your spending pattern, analyse your bank statements and understand where your money is going. Some may even be paying for services they no longer need, without knowing, yet going around begging for food. You may be able to find an alternative that could help improve your situation. If you are happy to hold on to tradition even if it no longer benefits you, you should welcome the consequences and the impact on other areas of your life.

Why should you *Close-up* when you have the power to *flourish?* Choose to set yourself free.

WHY SHOULD YOU *CLOSE-UP* WHEN YOU HAVE THE POWER TO *FLOURISH*?

Chapter 10

THE VIRTUES OF TENACITY

The story of everyone is different, so also are the challenges each one has to face. No one cap fits all. There would be no more problems if there were a cap like that. Everyone has something unique about their situation. One may seem easy and another difficult. One may be over in minutes or days, while others may linger on for months or years.

We only often wonder why it takes longer, while it seems it takes a shorter time for others. It depends on your needs and what you want to achieve.

Time is a significant factor in the making of any good thing. Some may take less time while others more, but you need to understand the process to help you persevere for the outcome. Some of the things you need may require that you wait because it has to go through a complete process that takes time.

A tomato seed can begin producing fruits after about fifty days of planting, with an average lifespan of six months.[1] It is not so with blackberry, which may take up to two years, but can live up to fifteen years.[2] The apple or pear tree is also different. They do not have fruits until the fourth or fifth year of planting, but they can live for a hundred years or more.[3]

It depends on what you need. If you need a tomato, it may be easier to get but quick to disappear within a short time. Blackberry will not produce like the tomato; it might take slightly longer but gives you over a decade of fruits. If yours is an apple, it will take even longer, so you have to wait for long in the early years, but afterwards, you and others enjoy fruits every season for a century or more.

Every plant is different, and they also vary in the time it takes to begin fruit-bearing. The same way, the need of everyone differs. It all depends on who you are and what you desire to achieve. One may hope to fulfil a temporary enjoyment, while another could think of something that will perhaps endure for many generations.

You cannot change the nature of the plant; you can only change your desire for it. If you cannot wait for the apple, you can opt for tomatoes. If you insist on an apple, encourage yourself to persevere and wait for it. Sometimes, many people desire apple fruits but never realise how long it takes to bear fruit. They look around them and see tomatoes everywhere. They wonder: 'Why is my apple not bearing fruit, while many tomatoes have good yields?' It is not yet time for the apple to bear fruit, you need to keep working on it, and the fruit will appear when the process is complete.

A student learns for over 14years in the tertiary institution to become a specialist in a particular area of medicine. Another may study for 7years to specialise in a specific type of law. Many other courses will not take that long, but they will not lead to medicine or law. All you need for your journey to become a specialist medical professional is to persevere through those years, seeking all necessary assistance till you achieve your goal. The time will come when you will eat the fruits produced every season, for many years to come.

It is vital to understand your goal and seek help accordingly. You may have found that not everybody will appreciate it. It becomes more challenging when it is not producing fruits like others you see around. There is help, but you need to seek them carefully throughout your journey to achieve your goal.

You may have chosen to raise a family. It comes with challenges and many needs. It may seem that you are behind in some things, but you are investing in a future. You are contributing your quota to the success of the next generation. You may have to deny yourself some things or always looking for someone to help you with one thing or the other. You cannot make it faster, but you can get help on your journey to achieve your goals.

Some people desire to start a business which may be a good goal. It involves a lot of work and investment of time to make it successful. Some have had to deprive themselves of pleasure and comfort to make their business a success. They have needs, but they understand why, and they are willing to persevere to realise their goal. It is a season. If you are doing what is required, you will soon see your fruits in the harvest season.

I know of some people that left their salaried jobs to start up their own business. They expected success so early, but they never realised all that was required. It requires more than what they put into their former jobs. They now need to look for clients, manage the business, pay for employees, pay for utilities, pay for other expenses, and so on. They can only think of profit after paying all the bills.

Do you have a goal, and it seems it is taking forever? Try to understand it and seek help as required to know what it takes to get there. Please do not give up on your goal because of the time it will take. Learn to persevere and seek help on your journey so that you can achieve it.

You may have chosen a more challenging path. You must understand the intricacies of your choice. Be willing to pay the price for what you desire. It may not be as easy as others, but it could be that the fruit will be worthwhile compared to others. The tree may endure for many generations.

Are you on the verge of giving up? Do you seem to be behind when others are progressing? It may be that you have different destinations. It could be that you are growing different trees. When you are enjoying your fruits, they may need to begin another round of planting all over again. Do not give up! You may be the hope for the next generation.

Chapter 11

THE VALUE OF UNTAPPED RESOURCES

It is challenging enough to be in need, but the solution is also not an easy one. You may find that you have to do something inconvenient or move out of your comfort zone, think differently, do what you have never done before, or do more than you have ever done to effect a change.

Most often than not, we have expectations and desires that everything happens as we hope. It does happen sometimes, but not all the time. Those that enjoy such may consider themselves lucky or probably good planners. The problem arises when it does not work as planned or failed after it had once succeeded. You may have been there. Some become blank, no knowing what to do because there seems to be no other way.

Have you heard people say things like 'I do not have any money' 'I have lost everything' 'Everything is gone' 'It is all over' 'I do not have anything'? It may be a reaction to a loss, failure or an unpleasant experience. I wonder if the statement truly represents the situation. Some even go a step further to declare that 'I will kill myself.' It is a feeling that there is no hope. It is like saying that it is better to die than to be alive or that there is nothing of value left.

I do not know of anyone that would receive a million pounds and accept to get killed instantly. 'How would I enjoy the money?' That would probably be the argument. In other words, the money is good, but my life is still valuable. I can still have opportunities, do things, discover new things, meet new people, find new ways, realise my errors and so on. It implies that the individual considers life worth more than money even when there seems to be none visibly. The truth is that there is something of value left as long as there is life.

The time of need could be frustrating, but it could also be a time of great opportunities. It seems that challenges attempt to blur the vision and cloud the mind. It makes it difficult to see clearly and think productively. You may discover that you have much more than you could ever imagine, but you do not realise it because you have never put them to use.

Imagine a businessman that lost his business. He says I have nothing. If you ask him, you will probably discover he has more but probably does not know they are valuable and could help him. Does he have anything? Yes, He is alive; he has time, gifts and skills. His environment is full of resources including, friends, families, colleagues, possessions and many more. We often despise what we have and decide to give up because of an unpleasant situation. What you have could be put to wise use—it could be the help you need to get back on track.

An employee that lost her job could use her time for so many things. A lady once lost her job in a company. She got an idea to use her resources. She used her time, kitchen and some raw materials—in her house, to make cookies and took them to the same company. It was a treat that generated so much positive feedback. It did not end there. Someone spread the news around to another company that contacted her to provide catering services. It was not too long afterwards that the business expanded beyond what her small kitchen could handle. She could then afford industrial equipment and employed people to help her. She lost a job, but she had many other things. She used some of those untapped resources, and she was better off in no time.

I know a man who had a business idea, but he did not have enough funds to start. He decided to raise money by using his time, energy and skill to work for a taxi company until he could raise enough funds. He left the company after raising enough money and started his business. He became an employer soon after because his business required more hands because of expansion. He had what it takes to get what he needs but only realised when he decided to change.

Have you ever thought of what you have when in need? Have you imagined what you can do? Many people have an idea that needs one million pounds to start, and it will usually have a forecast that will generate one hundred million. It is good to have it, but where will you get the money? You may have heard people say things like: 'If only I can get one million, I will start a business and employ ten people.' Everybody can do that if they have the money, but the problem is that you do not have the money. Consider what you have and how you could use them to progress from where you are now to where you desire to be.

Time is the greatest asset available to all human beings. It is free and equal. It can help make significant changes to your situation. You can use it to develop yourself, to become a better person. You could gain knowledge, training, experience, exposure and connections by investing time wisely. Many people looking for work in a particular field do volunteer their time. They gain trust, experience, exposure and relevant contacts. They may get a job through the process or somewhere else, having gained confidence and skills through the process of using their time wisely. They had what it takes, but they only got what they wanted by using what they had.

There are so many things you have that could be of help to you temporarily or otherwise. A thorough assessment may prove revelatory as you may have found out that you could meet your needs with what you have. You could probably provide services for yourself or others.

You do not have a job, but you take your child to a child care centre and pay for the service. You take your children for extra lessons in a couple of subjects. You pay for contractors to clean your carpet, furniture and windows. You pay drycleaners to help with your laundry. If you have the time and skills required or can develop them, you could have some income by providing those services.

The reason why such professional services are more expensive is that you are paying for their valuable time. If you learn how to do it and choose to do it, you can get paid for your time. Many people that use such services do make much more money with their time, thus prefer to give it out to others as they would earn more within the same time. Your situation may be different at this phase of your life; if you are struggling and your time is not fully engaged, you may want to reconsider your decision and use your situation to your advantage.

Many people could recover from a crisis by following this principle. You may not even need to ask for help from anyone. Look around and evaluate what you have and how you could maximise the use for your progress. Many great people or businesses experience more failures than we get to know, but they approach their needs differently. They know what to do to get back on track, and they waste no time doing it.

A family once started a coaching centre, for which they needed students. They printed handbills, shared them among willing friends and families. They helped with the distribution in the neighbourhood to advertise the centre for several days. They also shared the news with word of mouth in their various networks. The result beat their imagination. They saved so much money— which they did not have in the first place using the resources they had in friends and family. The business started and grew with enough students to make it profitable.

Are you frustrated and rejected? Are you wondering: 'If only I had money, I would start my catering business'? You do not have money, but what do you have? Do you have time? Do you live in a house? Do you have a kitchen? Do you have an oven? Do you have some flour and other ingredients? Do you have some friends, neighbours, families, relatives, or colleagues? You may have discovered that you have enough to start. Start from where you are; start with what you have got, and grow from there.

Many people in life did not experience significant success until they made the most of what they had. Waiting for something great to happen while doing nothing may result in a waste of your time. You have not lost everything, even if you have lost some; there is something of value in you and around you awaiting full utilisation. It may be the key you have long-awaited to make progress. Please find it and put it to use.

Chapter 12

LEARN FROM OTHERS

The difficulties you are facing in life could be daunting. They may happen at different phases and leave you with a change that is beyond your control. You may not know what to do, but that does not mean that you have to live with it—there could be help available that you have not yet known.

Everyone has to go through some difficult situation at one phase of life or the other. Although some may seem better than others, no track in life is free of hurdles. We all need help, yes, at different stages of our lives.

It may be comforting to know that the problem you have today is similar—if not the same, to the one someone else had yesterday. If you are hungry today, many people have had that experience in the past. If you have lost your job, many others have had the same experience as far back as people began to get jobs. If you failed an examination, you are not the first. It has been happening from the time people sat for examinations. Do you lack money? You are not alone; it has been that way since the first printed note. It moves from hand to hand by voluntary or involuntary transfer until some have and others lack.

It is also interesting to know that the problems are similar and repetitive. Some of the basic needs of any human being include food, drink, clothing and shelter. It is not just for people living today; it has always been a need, and it will continue that way. It is worthy of note because it can help you in the search for relevant answers.

Some people have already gone through challenging times—they have a result, whether good or bad, based on their response at the time. It presents an opportunity to understand their situation, what they did or did not do and their resulting outcome. In other words, we already know the result of their actions; if we decide to do the same, we are likely to get the same result. If their responses brought about a positive change, a repeat of it within the scope of a similar circumstance would produce the same outcome.

One of the reasons I found mathematics exciting is because you can predict the outcome. If you follow the example carefully, using it as a guide, and apply the new figures in the correct context, you can be sure whether you are right or wrong. The same is true in life. There are so many examples we can learn from in times of need. We may not necessarily do what they did, but we could understand the result of what they did and decide to follow suit or otherwise.

Many people do not know what to do in challenging times, and they never consider it necessary to learn from other people that have gone through similar experiences in life. Someone somewhere has gone through what you are going through now, and their story or actions could be of great benefit to your life.

A student that keeps failing a competitive examination, for instance, may not know the reason why others can score high marks under the same condition. If he attempts to learn, he may discover that they have mastered easier and faster methods of doing the same thing.

Have you been applying for jobs and never got an interview invitation? Many people have done that, but some have gotten jobs, and many have done it several times. They may have some details that you do not have, which could help you make progress. People that take time to learn may soon discover why they never got a job offer. They would usually have a change of opinion after applying the knowledge they lacked. Some may regret not acting sooner, as they have been wasting their precious time.

If you are struggling, do not wait for things to get better. Learn from those that are already successful at doing what you are about to do. They will have some information that could help in making a better decision. They could help you with the knowledge that would help you progress from the point of stagnation.

Many young people suffer in silence, frustrated, and confused as they go through the different developmental changes and phases of their lives. Many have gone through the same, and they have information that could help—use it to your advantage.

A boy grows to become a man, and a girl grows up to become a woman. The different stages of their natural growth and development are not new. Some men and women that you trust could provide help, guidance, and support through the process. They have gone through those phases, and they have many things to offer that can make your journey smoother. Your parents and many other people you trust could provide the help you need.

You may be struggling in your career or work. Many people have been in that career for years, and they had good and bad experiences. They probably also have lots of information on how they overcame the peculiar challenges they have encountered in the process. You may be experiencing one of those at present. They already have the answer because they had the same problem. It is wise to learn from them to find out how to progress in your journey.

Imagine a young apprentice or graduate that starts to provide services. He may encounter a problem that never came up in his few years of training. He then proclaims: 'I have never seen this before.' It means he needs help. If a more experienced professional in the field arrives at the scene, the professional would probably smile and say: 'It does not happen often, it is one of the strange situations, but this is what you have to do.' If you do not know what to do, it may be time to learn from those who know. It is not a time to give up but a time to seek help from those that know.

What is your need? Have you tried all you know and cannot see any positive change? You may want to consider learning from the example of other people. There are so many opportunities to learn, but you should also be cautious to ascertain that the source is trusted and the information is relevant to you.

Chapter 13

LEARN FROM THE PAST

The things we see today are, in some ways, the same as what has happened some time ago. It is also likely to happen again in the future. It may not always be the same way, but close enough to identify it as a reoccurrence.

History is full of occurrences that repeatedly happen. Many people that trade in shares know that the prices go up and down. It has always been so. It could be high one hour and low the next. If you are excited about the investment, you may buy it when high. You are likely to experience a price drop when people begin to sell. Some will sell like others out of fear but will have incurred a significant loss in a short time. Everyone may be selling, but not everyone is doing so at a loss. The knowledge of the past is helpful to make informed decisions, but the lack of the same has made others incurred losses out of fear. If you can discover a consistent pattern in the past, it may give you a clearer picture of the future.

An investor that has studied that pattern can be comfortable buying when the price drops to a certain level. The drop could be for many reasons, but he is at rest because he understands why. It could be because of the season, demand, changes and so on. Insight into the past patterns gives some assurances because he knows it will pick up again after some time.

Have you experienced losses and wondered why? Are you selling at a loss while others are making profits? Are you struggling where others are succeeding? Are you anxious while others are at peace? You might have missed something significant that others know. It could be the knowledge of the past.

The same is relevant to life. If you know how it has worked, it will help you manage your expectations and prepare accordingly. If you are expecting a baby, for instance, relevant information would be presented to you. One of them is that the pregnancy will last for about nine months. It has been proven so many times by so many people. If you have found yourself in the same shoes, it is unlikely to be different. Help is available for each of the different phases. The experiences of those that have already been there can be priceless, and you can make the most of it.

The peculiarity of the season means that there are so many things that will change. You cannot eat some foods that you desire. Some clothes you like to wear may have to wait. Activities you would have loved to do will have to go down the priority list. They may not be wrong but perhaps incompatible with the phase or season.

You may be going through a period of inconvenience or restrain because of what you are about to deliver. You cannot do all the things you used to do. Yes, but it is for a purpose and a season. You are about to birth a change. If you want to bring forth something new, the past may give you an idea of the price to pay. It has happened sometimes in the past, so some information that could help you go through the same situation is available for your benefit.

There have been several economic crises in the past. Some were able to survive, while some others were not fortunate. What can we learn? We can learn a lot. The answers to some questions will go a long way in providing solutions for those experiencing the same thing now and in the future. How it happened, why it happened, when it happened, the impact, what people did to recover, what to do to prevent a reoccurrence, and so on. The information would help meet future needs. It could prevent or reduce the impact in case of an inevitable occurrence. It is a significant help that is available that no one should ignore.

The same is true for disasters like floods, hurricanes, tsunami, epidemics, pandemics etc. If we learn more from history, it could help us better prepare and reduce the impact. The world has experienced so much and has provided us with a rich history. It will not only help to live better but also help to avoid the mistakes of the past. It is the way to maximise the opportunities of the future.

At the onset of the coronavirus outbreak that started in China, many nations reacted differently. Taiwan, a country very close to China, recorded very few deaths. The number was less than ten for over twelve months, even though tens of thousands of deaths occurred in many nations during the same period.[1] Many would wonder what they have done differently.

It is interesting to know that Taiwan is not even part of the World Health Organisation. It decided to implement a series of measures, such as screening, aggressive containment, quarantine, and monitoring from December 31, 2019. It was the day it learned of the virus, then unknown in the Chinese city of Wuhan. Why did such measures come to mind? You may ask.

I discovered that in 2003, Taiwan was among the worst-hit territories during the severe acute respiratory syndrome (SARS) outbreak claiming 181 lives. Taiwan's National Health Command Center (NHCC), set up during the SARS outbreak, represented the pool of resources and lessons from the past.[2] They responded so quickly because of the crisis they suffered in the past. They understood the implications and impact of a similar occurrence in the past. They went all out to prevent another one.

The past gave them the necessary information and sense of urgency to react to the signs of another similar outbreak. The nation once experienced loss; it could have happened again, but relevant measures were put in place to prevent it. Losses, on a larger scale, were averted by learning from the past.

Some eighteen months into the pandemic, they got complacent and saw a rise in deaths, but their record was still low compared to many other nations as they remembered the past and made amends accordingly.[3] The experience also becomes another lesson to help equip them for the future and prevent a repeat.

There are now so many similar initiatives in different nations to prevent such losses. Learning from the past prepares us to save the moment and the future from further loss. Whatever your need, you may find some clues in similar events that happened in the past that could help.

Please, do not neglect the past—It may be repeating itself. The more you learn from what has happened before, the less repetition of unpleasant experiences. You can make a difference by learning from the past because if you apply the lessons correctly, you will avoid the pitfalls and make fast progress in your journey in life.

Chapter 14

CONNECT WITH PEOPLE

One of the comforting things to discover in times of need is that you are not alone. There are many others in the same boat. You may get help quicker by connecting to those that have similar needs. There are so many problems in life and so also are solutions. You may be able to take advantage of current information from people that are also going through the same challenges.

A student writing a college examination may learn many things from those preparing for the same. It could be various information, including process, techniques, venues, registration, and correspondence, to mention a few. The journey could be smoother if the student has access to people undergoing the same process.

I heard the story of a university student that got admission to start a new course. She was new to the environment and the process. It was not like her secondary school, where students in a class stayed together for most of their subjects. What did she do? She found that many people were going towards the library, so she followed and stayed there to read, day after day and went back home afterwards. It seems, to her, like what every student does. One day, one of the workers noticed she is always in the library and decided to ask. Are you a new student? She answered in the affirmative. She then got some education on the process and where she needs to go.

The student probably was given information but probably ignored it or did not understand. It is also possible that she turned up late and missed important details. Many things could have been the cause, but if she could connect to some other new students in the department, it could have helped her find her footing easily—as they all have the same goal and would go through the same process. She could have confirmed that she was in the right place by checking those surrounding her.

A young man registered to sit for a series of examinations. He prepared alone and attended the venue to sit for each on the specified day. He relied on a calendar for the date, but unfortunately, it was incorrect. He did not turn up as the calendar mixed up the date and suggested the paper was for the next day. He failed. It was a painful experience, but if he was in touch with others doing the same thing, regular updates could have helped him. Someone in the group may probably also notice his absence and get in touch. The energy that drives a common goal could be helpful.

It is also applicable in other areas of life. If you are looking for a job, connecting with other people seeking the same could help you. You would be connecting to a pool of resources that aims to achieve a specific goal. You could gain speed because other people have the information you do not have, and your input could also benefit others.

An applicant may get a call for a job interview. He could share with others some tips on how he was selected. Another may be selected or rejected after an interview and could provide some vital information to others. Some could have a list of recruiting organisations or relevant opportunities. The list is endless. The more people that have the same goal, the more help they could be to one another. If you are always with people with different goals, you are likely to have more distractions. It will not contribute positively to achieving your goal.

There are so many ways to achieve this, including meetings, forums, groups, professional bodies, associations, one to one visits and so on. It depends on what is appropriate for you at every phase of life. I know of some groups for young mothers that meet together to share experiences and challenges they face. They share ideas to help with keeping the home or raising a specific age group of children. Mothers with babies may benefit from such ideas from other mothers with children of similar ages. Some may have toddlers; connecting to parents having similar challenges could help. They could also share new and current opportunities that are available, which are relevant to their goal. It could be child care, life-work balance, growth, education, and many others applicable to that phase of their lives.

Some people could be seeking scholarships, apprenticeship placement, university places, and so on. You are not the only one. They are many others that could be in the same position. You could benefit from relating with them.

You may be part of a group or forum, for instance. A member decides to decline a job offer or probably got a better offer from another organisation. He could be in a position to suggest a colleague. The information could be helpful to someone else that needs the job. The job may be open to the next candidate that also applied for it. If more people are required, he could inform people he knows that need such opportunity but not people he does not know. The person could be you.

You may need some legal assistance. Many people do. You can find forums that address the challenges or issues that require justice.

If related, the information will benefit more people with the same problem, thus helping more people.

You may ask, but if no such group is available near me or non-existent: what do I do? You can connect with people from anywhere around the world to get information, advice and support. The location should not be a barrier. There are also many resources documented by various forums that could benefit people that are having similar problems. It may not be live or active, but it could meet your needs. If none exist, you may start one. You may be the hope of many seeking help in that area. You will be surprised at the attraction of people that have such needs to your innovation. If it is happening to you, it is proof that many more people are going through the same or had or will soon do so. Seeking help as a group gives more strength to achieve the goal and lightens the burden. It is shared by many and not one person.

There are benefits to enjoy from other professionals by joining the relevant association or professional body. Carpenters can help one another in their trade. The same goes for electricians, traders, engineers, doctors, politicians etc. You benefit from a pool of resources to which everyone contributes. You do not have to do all the work, do your bit, and everyone enjoys the benefit.

You could benefit from updates, ideas, challenges, new policies, changes that affect your area of interest. You also have access to connections that could help you. The group members may have access to people or resources that could help you. What you need may be available to someone else but not particularly useful to them. They will be willing to give it to you if they know you.

It is vital to check that you are joining a trusted and reliable company. Find what works for you and be a part of the pool of resources to provide and or receive help in your chosen area of interest.

THE MORE PEOPLE THAT HAVE THE SAME GOAL, THE MORE HELP THEY COULD BE TO ONE ANOTHER.

Chapter 15

THINK BEYOND YOUR NEEDS

It is hard and challenging to be facing so many problems without knowledge of what to do. You may have found yourself in a position that you have needs with no idea how to meet them. Some sell what they have, especially the excesses and luxuries, to cater for vital or pressing needs. If the situation does not improve, they are likely to continue to sell more. It becomes disturbing to know that in some cases, everything they have and own, including themselves becomes available and can be offered or demanded in exchange for what they need. It seems they end up having no choice or right to anything at all.

The time of need is when you are at your lowest and most vulnerable. So many people know this and seek to take advantage of you and your situation. It is crucial to manage the situation well as you could avoid making things worse by proper management. Many seek to take advantage of the weak points in people and use it as an opportunity to rid them of their valuables, including their rights and dignity.

No matter how great your need is, you have the power to choose where you receive help. It is crucial because it may turn out to be a trap that could put you in bondage or one that could make you lose your rights, honour or dignity. You may need to ask yourself some sincere questions. Why is this company, person, group, or nation willing to help me? What are they expecting in return? Do I understand their aim or purpose? I know you may think of many more. You need the answers to help you make informed decisions before you jump for any offer of help.

Imagine a lady that did not do well at a job interview. she then gets a call from one of the recruiters, saying that they could help her get the job but in exchange for selfish gratification. It may look good as there is hope that she would get a job, but it is a trap that keeps people in bondage. You will probably do well by getting help to qualify for the post or look for another than getting it without merit and becoming a slave selling your rights, honour and dignity.

A lady was once offered help in time of need by a colleague. She willingly accepted it and appreciated the act. Sometime afterwards, the colleague came back asking for various favours from her. She was asking for what she could not afford, making demands on her resources and time. She obliges for a while, but it became inconvenient, and she felt bad as her friend reminds her of the initial favour every time she refuses her request. She thought she might have been better off if she did not get any help from her. It means different things to different people. Some people only help you because they hope to enjoy something you have or are likely to have. If you are not thinking the same way, there would be a big problem soon. You would both be disappointed.

A rich man may be interested in a poor talented young man. He invests in him to use his skill to expand his business. The young man may not understand why until he desires to be free and independent. He may be shocked at his findings. So many people have faced such shocking experiences. It is crucial to understand what you are getting into even if you have needs, as every help may not work for your ultimate good.

Do not give yourself away for trash; you are valuable even if you think otherwise at the moment. Value generates interest. If something has value, people get attracted to it. If people are attracted to something, it is because it has some value in their estimation. Some people lose the sense of value because they have a need. They sell themselves to meet their needs and find it difficult, if not impossible, to recover what they lost.

Have you ever wondered why some parents are willing to offer underage daughters to men in exchange for money? Why do some students offer themselves for grades? Why do employees sell themselves for a favour? It may probably be that someone else has more value for what they have than them, as they do not count it as anything of value.

If people cannot help you without taking advantage of your vulnerable situation, it is better to seek help elsewhere. You have the power of choice. In other words, you could refuse anything that has the potential of taking away your rights or dignity. It may be better to endure the challenges for a while than to subject yourself to many years of emotional torture, loss and pain.

Voters in so many countries get easily influenced by gifts and favours. They change their minds because of what they have received. They may probably get what they wanted for the moment, but they have lost their rights. They may have sold the future of the next generation because of need.

Many have abused the position of trust because of their personal needs. They have made right, wrong or wrong, right. They could not stand for the truth because of the favour they have received. They have done more harm than good to many.

A student once gave herself to satisfy her lecturer in exchange for good grades. She did not get what she wanted in the end. She was only used to fulfil a selfish desire. Many approach their needs the same way; they are willing to offer anything for it. The end is usually not as they may expect. They may realise that they have exchange value for trash.

Your needs are like dirt wrapped around gold. Many offer to help you so that they can give you something insignificant and take away your gold without you knowing it. If they are interested in your dirt, it may be because they have seen your gold.

It may not be a good idea to be desperate, willing to do anything and everything to get what you need. Do not just think about yourself or the present need. Think about how it affects others and the future. It is not just about getting your needs met; how is also vital. Please do not sell your rights; you may live to regret it.

Chapter 16

ALL I NEED IS HELP

The challenges of life could be overwhelming. It could even be more trying and frustrating if those that could help you misunderstand you. It could be worse if those that love you do not realise, thus hurting you more. Have you been in such a situation?

It would have been an ideal situation when you, those around you, or probably those that could help, know what you need and can assist. It is not always so, most often than not for some people. Many ended worse because they never got the assistance they required when they needed it. The problems we see stems from not knowing how to get support or a misunderstanding of the situation, in some cases.

Many years ago, my family lived next door to a young man. He looks respectful and would pass for someone that could not hurt a fly. It could only take living close to him to change your mind. He was struggling and frustrated. He was into drugs because of his past experiences and disappointments. He sought a different lady almost every week to stay with him. They were arguing, fighting, throwing furniture at each other, among other things, often. It was challenging to have a quiet night. He continually observed our family, and one day he decided to knock at our door. He saw a family, according to him, he desires. 'Is it possible for a family to be like this?' he thought. He was looking for something, but he never knew how to get it. He found an example of what is different or better than what he was used to—he got attracted as a result. He saw the possibility to live without doing the things he was doing.

His question baffled me. He asked, 'Are you human beings?' Yes, we are just like you, I answered. It occurred to me that he wanted peace, but he never knew how. He wanted fulfilment, but he did not know how to go about it. He did not want to hurt anyone, but he found no example to guide him. I was glad to help, showing him how we lived and what has made a difference in our lives. He realised that challenges are common to all, but knowing what to do at every phase of life makes the difference. He was willing to receive it and saw the difference. He decided against drugs and chose to start a new course of his life. He was eventually free from the addiction, began to think and live differently. He later got married and continued on the new path.

Have you ever wondered how many people are in a similar position? They only need an example to guide them on the right path. They need support on how to achieve their desired goal.

A woman that once changed to a man at sixteen revealed the damage it caused to her life. In retrospect, she regrets it, as she now agrees it was an uninformed decision. She joined a court case to protect others in a similar situation. She was excited that the high court judgment supported her position. She wished she got relevant assistance sooner. [1] All she needed was support to navigate through that phase of her life.

The security guards at a Whole Foods store caught a woman shoplifting and then detained her. The guards called the attention of the police because she has some stolen food in her bag, but the policeman did something different. The woman told him that she was hungry and that she had no money. He checked the bag and saw that it was just food and decided—along with his other colleagues, to pay the bill instead of arresting her. The woman was overwhelmed with emotion as she sobs into a tissue expressing gratitude.[2]

The thief may be someone that needs money but does not know how to get it legitimately. The prostitute may be one with emotional needs but does not know how to meet them. The adulterer could be someone deprived of joy or fulfilment but does not know how to go about it. The rebellious could be a child in need of affirmation but does not know how to get it. The loose girl may be the child deprived of fatherly love but does not know how to fill the gap.

The student constituting a nuisance may have failed in every attempt at doing everything he knows to do and does not know how to get on. The burglar could have tried to get work severally but failed and cannot see any opportunities. The trouble maker may be someone that cannot understand how others are doing well, and yet he cannot thrive in life. The dull child could be one with needs that nobody seems to understand.

The cheat could be one that failed his exams and does not know how to pass. The frustrated team member could perhaps, be someone different from others and does not know how to be happy with his uniqueness. The offensive neighbour could be frustrated but does not know how to solve her problems; then begins to think and do the unthinkable. The deceiver is probably someone deceived and robbed but does not know how to recover and decides to deceive others.

The restless child needs attention and understanding, but no one seems to be able to understand. The noisy colleague could be someone that desires to be heard, hurting but does not know how to get assistance.

If you can hear their cry, if you can feel their pain, if you understand their frustration, they may be saying nothing more than these five words; '...all I need is help'.

Evil increases when people have needs they do not know how to meet. Dissatisfaction has made many hate themselves, preferring to be like someone else. A relevant example or support would go a long way to help appreciate their uniqueness.

When people do not know how to get assistance, the problem multiplies. They may lose hope, call it quits, venture into evil, or some others become suicidal. All that is required is access to the relevant support. When people know what to do and are willing to do it, they can meet their needs. They have the opportunity to maximise their potential. The reverse is also true. If they do not know how to get access to the assistance they require, it may affect their lives negatively and that of others. It explains why many are in the position they find themselves in today.

What you are going through may not be strange, but it may be unfamiliar. You will do well to seek the support that is relevant to your situation. You may also be in a better position to support those in need. The signs you see around you as a leader, teacher, parent, manager, or president may be one revealing their needs and struggles, not their wish. All they probably need is help.

Chapter 17

UNDERSTAND THE BONDS

Everyone that needs help would be excited at every opportunity to get the help they need. Have you ever thought of the experiences of those that offer to help?

Many people have had unpleasant experiences in a bid to help. It may have affected some, but others have persevered in doing good regardless of some disappointing experiences. However, it is very crucial not to mismanage the contributor-beneficiary relationship. Treating those that help with respect will encourage them and also increase their willingness to do more. Some people are in need because someone abused the privilege of help and robbed many others of the same.

An employee that lost his job or one with challenges in business may approach some friends, colleagues or neighbours for a loan. They gave him what he requested, but also terms and conditions to guide the relationship. The employee signed the document, took the money and began to use it.

Eventually, his circumstances improved, and the loan was due to be repaid either totally or gradually, but he decided to renege on the agreement. He was out of reach and became uncontactable. They helped in the time of need, but they now have to be chasing him to get their money back. He was always available when he needed help but out of sight after he got helped. It is not a wise thing to do.

It is crucial to respect the terms and conditions of the relationship. Remember, they helped in your time of need. It is only respectful to honour the agreement to which you were both bound. If anything has gone wrong, let them know, you may get more help than when you disappear. If you cannot keep the agreement, do not receive the support.

Many people want to dictate the conditions, but they never realise they are the ones in need of help. The bank that lends you money dictates the agreement. They set the amount of minimum repayment every month. If you need their assistance, it is on their terms, not yours.

If you borrow a car, it is only reasonable to respect the terms of the owner. You have a need, and they have decided to help you; you should respect their terms otherwise seek support elsewhere.

I once offered a lift to a stranded young man. He was a smoker, but that was not a problem. He wanted to smoke in the car with me. I said that I am happy to give him a lift to his destination, but he would not smoke in the car because I do not smoke. If you need help, you must appreciate that people give you what they have and not what you expect them to have.

I have heard people complain about those that help them, but most often than not, their disappointment is because they want to impose their terms or preferences on those that want to help. If you need help and people are ready to assist, it is wise to honour them by respecting their terms. If you cannot respect their conditions, do not get their help.

If you got free accommodation, the owner expects you to keep it clean. Some may consider it strange, but he only expects you to keep it the same way he would or the same way he expects you to if it were yours. He is not making any money from you, but you are using his property. If you cannot make it better, do not make it worse.

A family may welcome you to their home to help you in time of need. They provide food and shelter. They may decide to give you as much liberty to make you comfortable, but you should not forget that they deserve to be respected, and you cannot impose your preferences on them. They could be happy to accept your choices, but you should not abuse the privilege. They are only helping you.

Some young people frustrate the efforts of their parents. They live with their parents, eat free food, pay no bills, and desire to dictate for others to follow. They gave you liberty, so you have a sense of belonging but should not be abused. You have rights but remember someone else is taking responsibility for you, bearing a cost that you cannot yet afford and shouldering risks on your behalf. They deserve that honour.

If you become independent and do not need them, you can exercise your rights as you like. In most cases, parents labour so hard to give the best to their children. It is not wise to despise their efforts.

You may have always enjoyed an affluent lifestyle, but when there is a change in your circumstances that means you need support from other people to survive, you should learn to adapt. A friend or relative decides to help, but he may not afford the same lifestyle. If you are not happy to enjoy what he has got or can afford, it is better to leave him alone. He is only helping you.

Many helpers have been frustrated because of people that do not have understanding. We know you were rich, but everything has gone pear-shaped. You now need help, but the person helping you does not have the responsibility to maintain your former lifestyle. He can only provide what he can afford—to probably get you back on your feet or till you understand the lessons that made things change for you.

Some children complain so much about their parents. There is nothing good enough. They want everything, especially what others have. Most parents, if not all, will do their best for their children, but if you have not had a good experience, recognise that they are doing all they know to do to help you. Many only get to appreciate the sacrifices when they get to the position of responsibility. If you cannot take full responsibility for your life and actions, respect those that support you.

The government supports citizens to the best of their ability. Admittedly, some do more than others, but whatever they do is help and should be appreciated by contributing the required quota to fulfil civic responsibilities.

Are you the helper or the helped? You will do well to respect the agreement that binds you together.

Chapter 18

YOU ARE IN SCHOOL

Empowered with facilities, resources and speciality, school is one of the most palpable places recognised to provide education and development opportunities.

In many countries, it is compulsory to go to school, at least to a certain level. You probably have gone through such systems and have been educated in a particular field or profession.

I wonder what the answers of a hundred students would be when asked, 'why are you going to school?' The answers could vary, but one or more may answer, saying: 'I am going to school to learn.'

Sometimes, I ask students about their schoolwork and hear different responses. One answer could be as follows; 'We did word problems in Mathematics today. We had a lesson and then some questions afterwards, to which we were to apply the knowledge gained.' It is interesting to note that they went to school to solve problems.

There was once an upset student that did not like the idea of solving problems. He was frustrated about so many different things at different times. On this occasion, it was a word problem to solve after some lessons. The teacher read it as follows: Jude was given three pounds and fifty pence by his Dad, Jon, for his lunch money. On his way, he was running on the school field and lost seventy-five pence. How much did Jude have left?

Most of the students could relate the knowledge to the problem; a few asked related questions, while others found it straightforward. There was, however, one different reaction. One of the students was furious—thinking that he required assistance—the teacher asked; What is the matter? He responded, why did Jude run on the field? He should have walked carefully to avoid the loss. He has created a problem for us. We are now suffering for his actions. I wonder what you think of his response. It is interesting to know that there are different reactions to the same problem in the class.

It is similar in life because it is full of problems, and we all react differently. Every class has its problems with varying degrees of difficulty, but the idea is to learn to solve them. Frustration continues if we only avoid them or complain about them.

It is interesting to see that you have a lesson to learn from, then you are given related problems to solve to test your understanding. It is the opposite in life. You get the challenges before you learn the lesson that comes through the experience.

The best students in school usually spend so much time practising the problems, solving different types, and doing all the exercises. It is understandable, they are better, but they have invested more time, probably solving all possible questions that may arise, so they become a master in solving them. Their attitude then becomes different. They are happy to solve the problems, unlike the student complaining about Jude. Some students want the class to end because they do not understand how to solve the problem. The excited ones are those that know what to do.

The masters are usually those that faced their challenges and solved their problems. They were once broken but eventually, become a master at mending. They once tried, though failed but found how to succeed.

What are you going through? What is the problem or challenge before you? It may be the school you require to learn to be a better person.

Many successful people became great by attempting to solve their problems. They eventually became a master, helping others with ease and getting rewarded for it.

You may have a great business idea, but you do not have money. It is similar to a word problem. There is a known and unknown, how can you solve the problem. If you spend so much time researching a solution, you would soon become a master in doing so, thus opening the door of opportunities to help others. You will get a reward for inventing a new solution.

There is something similar in the biographies or autobiographies of most people that become successful. You will observe that there would be a problem or series of challenges in their stories, to which they found solutions. It could be poverty, lack, hatred, abuse, loss, deprivation, limitations, disorder, rejection, frustration, interruption, change, or detestation. The experiences through those times, most often than not, becomes instrumental to their success. They sought a solution to the problem and became a master in helping others. They usually pioneer a new career that flourishes on the victories of their experiences.

You may find that an orphan that becomes great starts an orphanage or provide opportunities for their benefit. An individual that suffered abuse would fight for justice for others or provide education for their liberation.

If you have failed an exam and later passed, you would appreciate success better and treat others in the same position with understanding. The lesson comes after the problem.

Many people are frustrated under leaders that cannot understand what their followers are going through because they have never been there. They have never had to solve such problems. They do not know how it feels.

A Research work that studied the data from 35,000 employees and workplaces provided some conclusions that suggest that if your manager could competently do your job, he is likely to treat you well and with understanding compared to those that cannot do or understand what you do.[1] Some lessons are learnt only by being in the same shoes or understanding how it feels.

Your situation may provide the education you need to make progress and improve. It may help you appreciate and understand others. It could be a pointer to a problem you could begin to solve. It may be your university to equip you for a new career. It could help you gain confidence, experience over the issues and circumstances as well.

Many organisations, nations and individuals spend so much on learning. Your need may have given you that opportunity with you knowing. If you take advantage of the opportunity, you could soon become a master—helping others find the way. Cheer up! You are already in school.

Chapter 19

TAKE RESPONSIBILITY

It is one of those frustrating and disappointing experiences in life, one that everyone would wish that it offers an opportunity to smile at last or a sigh of relief. It is a situation that you asked for help or expected one from someone you think could help, but you were wrong—they cannot help. You probably have had such an experience and know how it feels.

Sometimes we expect some people to help us. We get disappointed, but we may never realise that they cannot help or do as much as we desire.

I remembered one science experiment we did in school many years ago. It was to determine the elasticity of a material. An elastic material like a rubber band was among the requirements for the experiment. We had to hang the rubber band from a clamp stand and added a series of masses of 100g each on it, using a mass holder with a hook. A ruler clamped vertically is placed by the side to measure the distance. We took the initial measurement with no mass added. The 100g mass got added to the mass holder one at a time while observing, taking notes and recording the readings.

The more mass added, the more it stretches. You can add up to five or even ten or more and examine. Like so many other experiments, there are so many lessons to learn from the exercise. It shows the property of the materials involved. At a certain point, if you keep adding the mass, the rubber stretches that it cannot expand any further—what is hanging on it is now greater than it can bear. It snaps—all the mass drops.

It is an important lesson that applies to life. It is the concept of limit. Everyone has a limit, and we should appreciate individual characteristics and limitations.

You may assume that some people can help. Yes, they probably could. You may be like one of the 100g masses, not knowing they have reached their limit or are at breaking point. Yes, they have helped others in the past—you assume the conditions are still the same, but their present circumstance cannot accommodate any more. It may not be that they do not want to help, but they cannot. Some are in a broken state, but you may not realise.

I can understand the disappointment of so many people when they seek help from colleagues, acquaintances, friends and families. It may be that they have stretched beyond the limit. They may not tell you all the details, but they may not be in a position to help.

What do you do in such circumstances? Take responsibility for your life. Do not blame people or blackmail them. They probably have helped you sometime in the past. You need to rise and take up the challenge. So many people have resulted in blaming people for their misfortune. Children sometimes blame their parents, citizens of a nation blame the government, employee accuses the employer, one government blames another for their problems—it is always the fault of someone else.

It is vital to realise that they can only do so much. No one can give you what one does not have. Most parents do all they can to help their children. They are limited—they may have done their best or all they know to do. If you want to go any further, you must take responsibility for your life, appreciate all their efforts and accept their limits.

You have put your hope in people long enough, but they failed you. You need to rise and take responsibility for your life. Stop waiting for them to change; you can decide to make that change. Your teachers, friends, community, and colleagues may have failed you, but you can take steps to address the wrong. There is hope for tomorrow if you decide to change today.

You may have sought help and ended up worse or even have been robbed by those you once trusted the most. There is hope for you. Help is a privilege that you should appreciate. Everyone around can only try as much as they can. Some of the people that failed you may not have done so intentionally. Some in a bid to help have found themselves in a mess. It may not be their desire, but unfortunately, they did not know any better, neither did you, at least at that time—you could have made a better decision to avoid the situation. If you point one finger to blame others, you are pointing three towards yourself. It only implies that you have more responsibility for your life than anyone else.

If you attend a primary school, you will get all the help and support you need at that level. A time comes that you have to leave. You need to enter another stage of life. The assistance you get from primary school is no longer sufficient for your new phase of life.

You progress to secondary and get secondary level assistance. A time comes when you have to leave as well. The help you need changes as you make progress in life. You may be stagnated and frustrated because you are focusing on those that cannot help you. You may be looking up to the wrong people to help you.

Imagine you enrol in a music school for beginners and get on so well with everyone. You have mastered the level and may desire to progress to the advanced stages. It is a good idea, so you approach the school to express your interest. They may then remind you that though they appreciate your love for the school and teachers, their service is for starters—they cannot help you any further. It may be a disappointment, but you need to go. You need to take responsibility and find out how you can progress your interest and desires.

A young child grows up with his parents with help and assistance to equip him for the future. A time comes that the child matures, and the support available cannot be the same as the younger years. There is a need to expand, start his own family, a need to manage his affairs, a need to become a parent, among others. He needs to take responsibility and learn to be independent. It is a new phase of life. You have to leave their house—where you got help, to begin to take care of yourself and raise others as well.

Whatever situation you find yourself in today, you need to assess your circumstance and seek a way to move forward. Let the past be gone, and look forward to the opportunities that lie ahead of you.

Chapter 20

THE CURRENCY OF TRUST

Endowed with a value that empowers with a firm belief in the reliability, truth, or ability of someone, trust is one of the most potent media of exchange in times of need.

Have you ever wondered why some people get help while some others struggle to get assistance? I have found that trust plays a significant role in the support we receive. It is like a currency in your bank account—when you have it in sufficient quantity, you can readily exchange it for what you need. However, some people make careless withdrawals and never realise that they have run of the currency. They are left without purchasing power when they need it most.

So many people find help and do so continually, most often than not, because of trust. Conversely, many that struggle to get help probably have run out of the currency of trust.

Many years ago, as a young boy, I had an experience that gave me a clear understanding of trust. There was a woman across the road to us that operates a small grocery shop. I usually visit the store to buy groceries and have done so for many years. One day I went to buy a loaf of bread as usual, but the regular size was not available, so she suggested that I take the next size up, which meant a price increase. As I did not plan for that, the money I had was not enough, so I explained that I would not mind following her advice, but I do not have enough money.

I decided to go home and return with the extra funds to make up for the complete payment before I took the loaf of bread away. I explained my decision, but the response I got blew my mind. The woman responded, 'No, do not worry about the money. You can take the bread now and bring the money whenever you are coming next.' I was quiet and thought about the situation carefully, wondering what could have been the reason behind such action.

I declined that offer—I went home to take the money to pay her before I took the loaf of bread, but the lessons stayed with me. She said these words; 'I know you, I trust you, I am sure you will bring the money.'

I got two lessons, among others which are as follows: Firstly, I was not doing anything deliberately to impress her, but she observed for a period to form an impression of me based on how I behaved to her and probably others. Secondly, I discovered that if I were in actual need, I have some 'funds' waiting in the bank of trust that could help me.

Many years after, I still found it to be true. I have utility contracts, and they write me to offer upgrades or other services because 'you are a trusted customer'. Banks write to me stating that they are happy to lend me money, with different offers and attractive rates. I found it is because of trust evident in our relationship for many years. Although I decline in most cases, it only shows that if I need it, I can get one because the relationship of trust made it possible. Instead of using it up, I keep adding to it, so more people and organisations are willing to help me. It is a function of trust.

Many people do not realise the value of trust. They cheat other people to get quick gain or defraud organisations that provide them goods or services. They refuse to pay their bills or dues—they run away from their creditors. They renege on agreements and refuse to honour their contracts. It may be little or much—it may be between you and a friend or perhaps an organisation. You may never know how it will affect you in future. It is worth investing in the currency of trust.

Many complicate their problems with dishonesty. They deceive, frustrating people that helped them, but they never realise that they have shut so many doors against themselves in the future. When you borrow money from a friend, and you refuse to repay—ignoring the person—you are gradually reducing your chances. You may have won once by cheating him, but you may have lost ninety-nine times in terms of future opportunities.

You may have enjoyed the services of a company in the past, but you failed to pay for it after satisfactory completion. You are losing your chances for help and reducing their willingness to offer such to those in need. There are times when some people cannot genuinely keep the agreement for circumstances beyond their control. It is better to keep them informed as you may get more options than to run away, deceive or ignore.

There are so many organisations or businesses that have benefited from relationships of trust for growth and development. They approach the bank for small capital for a business idea, and they keep to the terms and return the funds as agreed. They later ask the bank to get more funds—the bank gives more because of trust in previous dealings. Many have weathered difficult seasons because of the confidence built in their relationships in good times. A history of consistency in this currency may help you in the time of need.

Many people could get help from friends, colleagues or relatives, but they ruined such opportunities because of their past dealings. It probably was full of inconsistencies, deceit, dishonesty, failed promises, or contempt.

Many people are willing to sacrifice for those that are trustworthy. Some became weary because of some of the unpleasant attitudes and experiences. It takes a lot to screen or differentiate between the fake and the genuine in many cases. Many organisations invest so much to check for trust and credibility. It is the reason for credits checks, background checks, security checks, history checks, and references.

Some people have lost great opportunities and positions because of some inconsistencies in their history. A dishonest gain—no matter how much money is involved; is not worth it in the long run. Invest in the currency of trust before you have a need, you may never need to use it, but it is worth the investment. It is wise to keep a good history— it will help you when in need. Pay your dues, and do not defraud other people. The lifestyle may help you stay out of problems, but it also gives you a sense that people are willing to help you in times of need.

What is your situation today? Do you have funds of trust or lack them? You can turn over a new leaf and begin a change for the better if the latter is the case. If yours is the former, you could explore opportunities available through your relationships if you need help. If you do not need it, continue to add value by earning the currency of trust.

Chapter 21

THE VALUE OF CONTENTMENT

Need is one thing that is common to all. The need of one may be different from another, but everyone lacks something and requires help to get it. However, there is a bait that attracts many outside of the comfortable boundary. It is the desire for more. It could be for something extra that is not a need or probably what others have, but they do not yet have.

The desire to have more may promise a false sense of satisfaction, but many often discover it was probably a trap. It seems that more brings more dissatisfaction and more desire for more. There is no end to it. The poor want more; the rich want more—it will never be enough; it will never stop. It is a desire that cannot be satisfied; it is a race that has no finish line.

An employee with no car may be excited when he gets his first car. After a while, he is dissatisfied—he wants another one, and then another one. The thought that the newer car will bring satisfaction only lasts for some time, after which a current, better, more expensive one becomes the desired. It can still meet the need for transportation, but he longs for something more even when he cannot afford it. It is like a continuous cycle that never seems to end. Many have ended up in debt and frustration because of such a way of life.

Contentment will help you appreciate what you have and what you can afford. It will help you focus on what you need and use what you have for the correct purpose for which you need it.

We all go through different phases in life. It is crucial to understand this as many people desire to be like others but never know their history. Your friend could be driving an expensive car, but he might have come a long way. You may be comparing yourself with his life now, but he has gone through different phases and challenges in life. You may not be there yet, but trying to be like him now may even prolong your journey.

It is so interesting to see how many people live their lives. They desire to be rich but make themselves poor and make the rich richer. The desire to have more before the required time drives them to poverty—it only helps the rich people become more prosperous.

A worker that cannot afford an expensive car will buy one with a loan. He will have a luxurious car, but other areas of his life will suffer from that decision. He is becoming poorer—with a posh car—on loan. Guess what?—He will buy it from the rich and get the loan from the prosperous. So invariably, his decision has made the rich comfortably richer and himself poorer. He could have continued using his car, and probably he would be in a comfortable position to change it without affecting other areas of his life in future.

Consider someone that spends so much on luxurious items to impress other people but does not eat good food or take care of his health. He may soon become sick, which implies that he will require the help of a specialist to get his health back in shape. In essence, he will make someone else richer because of his decision.

Many young people spend so much on expensive clothes which they cannot afford. They run into problems because their appetite for such things grows uncontrollably, but there is no financial base to support such a lifestyle. The decision to maintain that standard means they have to deprive themselves of so many things to impress. They lose the little they have to make others richer. If they were happy with the clothes they could afford, they could progressively grow and become comfortable without any undue burden.

There are so many people and organisations that profit from those that are not content. The organisations enjoy profit increases when people keep buying what they do not need to satisfy a desire that will never be satisfied. They are happy with such decisions, but some people never realise that it is not advantageous in the long run. It is making them poor and someone else richer.

They may offer you newer, better and faster gadgets while the old one still fulfils the same purpose for which you bought it. You may have a sense of compulsion that you must change it even when there could be more important things that you could invest in, but remember that some are going to the bank smiling because of your lifestyle while you may be struggling to make ends meet.

You may have gained the freedom to do whatever you want. You decide to eat uncontrollably, feasting on sugar, sweets and chocolate. Soon your teeth may tell you that you need to give some of your money to the dentist. You will book an appointment and willingly take your money there. You are making the dentist richer by your decision. It is simple—the dentist will have his needs met by your decision while you will have more necessities to handle.

Some people may find joy in eating without control but afterwards spend so much to reduce the weight they have gained in the process. Too much of anything, even good things, could harm. Many have ignored the caution on the dangers of sugar for several years, but now they have to spend money to treat the repercussions. It is a great discipline to be content—to know when to stop, be happy with what you have and what is good for you.

Many people borrow as well as spending the little they have on get-rich-quick schemes and investments. They lose the money to the rich and now need to pay off the loan, making them more indebted—more trouble. Imagine a family that borrows a million pounds with a promise that it will double in about six months if invested in such schemes without doing anything. In the end, it fails—the money is lost, they are now one million pounds in debt. They were expecting to be millionaires, but now millionaires in debt. If they had not followed such ideas, they could have been in a better position. In mathematics, the number zero is more than any negative number, which implies that even if you do not have anything, you are better than someone owing without a means of repaying.

Some young adults do shady deals to get money to spend on things they see other people wearing. They get into trouble and need help. Some people may begin to contribute for their release or hire a legal expert for law proceedings. If they were content, they would have been in a better position. The desire to get more without following due processes and stages will usually bring more losses than gains.

Are you trying to impress by getting what you do not need or buying what you cannot afford? Are you enriching others to make yourself poor by your uncontrollable desires? Are you living a life that puts you at the mercy of others? Ask yourself sincere questions and make decisions that will help you and not destroy you.

Do you need more, or could you do with what you have and plan for your future so that you are not just meeting your needs but comfortable enough to help others as well? You can choose to make a difference, and many might also decide for a positive change, turning over a new leaf because of you.

You are on a journey; you can make tomorrow better because of what you do today. Be happy with the stage or phase of life that you are in at the moment and make progress at your own pace.

CONTENTMENT WILL HELP YOU
APPRECIATE WHAT YOU HAVE AND WHAT
YOU CAN AFFORD.

Chapter 22

Go the Extra Mile

One of the things we do not have equally is the opportunities and the privileges we enjoy in life. Some people have a better start in life than others, but many things contribute to our starting point. Many found themselves farther behind, while some found themselves with a silver spoon in their mouth. How can you journey in life from where you are to where you need to be, especially when you are not among those on the front line?

Life is like a race but with everyone in different starting positions. You may have found yourself farther away from others—you may lack what others have or may not have access to what some other people have access to in life.

Some people lost one or both parents while they were young. Some did not have access to free or private education. For some, they never had to work while they were young—the opposite for some others. Some never knew where meals would come from daily—they had to fend for themselves. Some had constant challenges at home that became a distraction that frustrated everything they attempted.

Some had to handle challenging relationships that affected their state of mind. Some did not have access to the right counsels and guidance. Some did not have materials that could help them make the right decisions. Some were victims of a government, some victims of a bad policy. Numerous are the challenges people go through, and it does affect their journey in life.

What do you do if you find yourself in such a position? What are your choices? Is there any hope? Do not give up—it is not the end. You may not be in the best position, but it does not mean you cannot fulfil your dreams. All it means is that you need more strength, courage and help to go that extra mile.

You may need to work harder to change your story. Some people do not have access to education—they had to compete with thousands or even millions to get a scholarship. It is hard work—it is going the extra mile. You cannot afford to copy others because there are not in the same position as you. You need to read more, study more to get such opportunities. It requires doing all you can to make that change happen.

How hard you need to focus and work depends on where you are. Many people do not realise this—they copy others that do not have similar challenges or experiences. They later discover they cannot catch up as they need to run twice as much—not at the same pace, to make a difference.

Many have overcome their limitations by working harder for opportunities, scholarships, funds, loans, and employment. A student that does not do well in Mathematics, for instance, probably does not have a good understanding of the subject. He may have gaps in his knowledge that have made it difficult for him to learn at the same pace as others.

It does not mean he cannot do well—it only means he needs to read more, do more to catch up with others. He may need to get relevant books, read more, borrow more materials, waste less time and focus on the subject. It is not a good idea to feel inferior or incapable, especially when others are doing well. You need to understand your situation and work harder to improve it.

If you are struggling in any area of life, it may be that your past has not prepared you for such challenges. It does not mean that you are strange, but a sign that you need to work extra on such areas to catch up. It may be easier for some to do well in the workplace, but for some others, they may have more challenges to deal with—affecting their performance. It means that they need to work harder and do more to achieve the same or better results.

A student that struggles to pass an examination may have found it challenging. However, spending more time studying relevant materials and for extra coaching will probably help him do better. Everyone can do well, but many factors that affect performance are not considered or worked on for improvement. A child with learning difficulties can do well with extra materials and attention. If left alone without further assistance, the challenges will affect performance and the result of the child.

If you start a new company from scratch, you may need to work harder to succeed. There are some things that you need to put in place that will require extra work and time. Established brands or those rebranding or merging may not need to do some of those things as they already have those privileges. They may have a structure, sponsors, customers, properties, a known brand, good history, and assets. It implies that they are starting on a better platform. A new company can achieve the same or better, but they would be prepared to work harder and do more. If you know the tasks ahead of you and your present position, you will understand the journey before you and prepare according.

If you were not born to an affluent family, it does not mean you cannot be wealthy. It only means you have to work harder and smarter. Many people seek better opportunities in companies or nations. It is not impossible, but it depends on where they are, compared to where they aspire to be in the future. They might need to work harder and go the extra mile to secure the opportunities they desire.

Many employers go to universities to select the best students—it is often a competitive process. Those that desire such plan ahead to work and burn the midnight candle to secure a juicy appointment—if they are not part of the selected few, they would have added value to make them competitive in other opportunities.

Many poor and less privileged have risen above barriers by taking advantage of such opportunities. The opportunities are there but will not literarily go to them, so they have to compete for it with hard work. You are poor does not mean you cannot be great—it only means you have to work harder than those with such privileges.

A politician that is not known could win an election, but he has to do more to gain the trust and confidence of the people. Opportunities come with responsibilities. If you do not have the best position, you can rise to work harder to change your story.

Some entrepreneurs borrow money to start a business. They need to make more than the loan to make a profit. As they do not have the initial funds, they have to work twice as hard to make money to pay off the loan and get some profit for themselves. They could work as much as eighteen hours a day to make a difference that will change their situation—some have changed their stories as a result—they now have enough money.

Many sportsmen and women work so hard to break through into the limelight. It does not just happen—they go the extra mile to make a difference. They are unknown, so they have to work harder to qualify and prove that they deserve a chance. They usually engage in rigorous and continuous training to develop and enhance their skills.

Some people may desire some job opportunities but may not be selected. They may have to offer their skills to big organisations as a volunteer. It may not produce profit immediately, but it may secure opportunities that will pay off in future. You may need to go that extra mile to initiate the change that you desire.

You can decide to change your situation by a deliberate and conscious decision. Do not give up! Do not let your circumstance overwhelm you. Go the extra mile to initiate a change for the better.

IF YOU ARE STRUGGLING IN ANY AREA OF LIFE, IT MAY BE THAT YOUR PAST HAS NOT PREPARED YOU FOR SUCH CHALLENGES.

Chapter 23

IN NEED OR WANT?

There are so many things one desires in life. Some are needs—the necessities for living or wants—they are those things that one desires but could probably do without and still be alive and well.

Sometimes some people treat need as want and want as a need. They may long for what they can do without, ignoring the necessary things to keep them alive and well. The classification may vary depending on individual preferences and goals, but if you desire help, you must ensure that the situation represents a genuine need.

It is not wise to take help or helpers for granted. Some have seen it as an easy way to get all their desires and pleasures. You may have heard of stories of beggars that gather money from givers and use it to build estates or buy other things in a different location so that the donors do not get to see or suspect their behaviour.

Everybody desires to progress in life to meet their needs and have more—for many different and variable reasons. It could be to accumulate more, or for comfort, get more things, execute plans or help others. However, it should not happen by deceiving people giving the impression that you lack necessities that could threaten your existence.

Some people mention their needs, and you feel so much for them, but their action or plans afterwards leaves you baffled. How can someone with such a need a few days ago be doing some significant spending a day after on something that is not a necessity? It could be confusing or probably surprising.

Some may tell you that he is broke, which means that he has run out of money. It implies that he does not have money for even his necessities. In that case, anything that could help the situation will be accepted and appreciated. In some cases, those that assist such people—even out of their little resources may get a feeling they have done nothing because those helped see their assistance as insignificant—not appreciated.

Furthermore, they now begin to buy things they could probably do without, which makes the helpers think and become surprised—I thought you were in need, but it does not look like it. Seeking help should not be an opportunity to take advantage of other people. It is a privilege you enjoy when you are down, and there seems to be nothing to keep you going. It is worth appreciating every effort to help and not act like an ingrate.

Let us consider another scenario where such individuals—that are broke—begin to spend on purchases that make them pass for comfortable people. It gives a different picture, and those that can help or have helped may become astonished.

Many people have always needed help because of the way they treat needs and wants. Some borrow to buy wants—the wants give them temporary pleasure—does not generate any income. They will soon have to seek more to continue to satisfy their pleasures.

You can get help for what you need to survive. You can also seek help for what you need to be independent or keep your work or business running; so you do not remain in the same situation. Some people always ask for help—they have received money and assistance several times, but they spend it on wants, not needs, so they eventually need to seek help again.

A young man that lost his job and ran out of money may receive some money. He could use the money to meet his basic needs and invest some into ventures to gain his source of income instead of using it to purchase some of the things he has long desired to own.

An employee made redundant could use his last pay and other assistance towards his basic needs and efforts to get another source of income instead of using the funds to go on his favourite holiday for pleasure. A family with insufficient income may get assistance to help with their necessities. They can work towards other sources of income instead of undertaking liability projects that they could probably do without or do later.

If you pour your efforts, time, and resources into your goal, business or vision in your time of need, it could end up generating more to take care of you in the future, but if you only think of the things you want and spend on those, you will probably always need assistance.

You can ask yourself sincere questions; Is it a necessity? Can I do without it and still be alive and well? Can I stop what I have always done and still be okay? If I do not get it, is something disastrous going to happen? The answers could help you in your classifications and decisions.

Some need money, but they spend so much on what they can avoid. There are so many things we do that have become a routine. We never think of changing them in time of need, but they form part of our outgoings and could be the source of savings. It could be a cup of coffee you buy from a restaurant every morning or lunch at a particular restaurant, or a favourite snack or a subscription for a service that you seldom use. It may be little things; yes, many little things can add up to become significant over time.

Every case may be different, but there may be something you could change, stop, or probably find a cheaper substitute so that you can navigate through the season of need gracefully. You can discipline yourself to maximise the resources that come your way. It is a conscious and deliberate effort that can preserve your future.

IF YOU POUR YOUR EFFORTS, TIME, AND RESOURCES INTO YOUR GOAL, BUSINESS OR VISION IN YOUR TIME OF NEED, IT COULD END UP GENERATING MORE TO TAKE CARE OF YOU IN THE FUTURE.

Chapter 24

THE MISPLACED PRIORITIES

Many people indeed have many things to do. For some, the list could be unending. However, at every point in time, one is usually more important than another. The struggles lie where many people find it challenging to pick one and leave another for later, or do one and discard the other, or re-arrange the order on the list. The impact of this decision is noticeable in the result. How do you organise your priorities to help you achieve your goal? How do you determine which is the most important at any given time?

It is your responsibility to determine what is important to you, but it is crucial to understand that the choice of doing one against another will vary the outcome you get at any point in time. If you do not do what is necessary to get what you need, you will still be in need. What you have done may have succeeded, but it is probably not what you should have done for the expected results.

If you spend all day watching the latest soap operas, you will probably be up to date and know more than those that have not watched it yet. You may realise that you do not have money at the end of the month because you did not work worthy of pay. What you have chosen to do is not necessarily a bad idea, but it does not provide you with money at the end of the day. If you are confused about why you do not have money, it is probably because of what you have made crucial and given the best of your time—it does not produce what you need.

Many have found themselves in need not because they were doing bad things but because they were doing good things that should be farther down on the priority list at that stage of their life. Many things look good, but depending on you and what you desire to achieve, they may have a place lower on your priority list.

A student committed to buying the latest mobile phone may have made that a priority over everything else. It implies that it is more important to get the phone first; he can then consider other things afterwards. If he ran out of money after buying the phone, he now requires probably food, transport or school materials. He will soon begin to beg for help.

You may need to decide how to use your limited funds and resources because many things are good and could equally compete for attention. It could be anything like new clothes, holidays, new cars, produce more products to fulfil customer requests, or home improvement, among others. They all look good, but with limited funds, you may not be able to do them all. A decision to do them in the order of importance is required to avoid ending up in need.

A family may need money for business, school fees, television subscription, new clothes for a party, new car, and house improvement. They are all good and genuine things to do, but which is more crucial when there is not enough to do all? If the car is more important than education, they can buy it and leave education till later. The benefits or consequences are a function of their choice.

If education is more important, they will push the clothes or car down the priority list to pay for education. It all depends on what is crucial. Some people may not have to borrow if they understand what is more important and treat it accordingly. The right decisions are necessary on every occasion. You may not afford everything, but you should know what is vital and give it its rightful place. Growth is gradual—you can grow at your own pace and make continuous progress.

Some people spend so much of their funds and later complain that they do not have any money for vital things in their life. An employee gets a paycheck and spends everything without planning. His house rent, utilities, transportation, or other necessities are still pending, and he has nothing left. He probably did not consider those as crucial, but they eventually put him in a difficult situation.

Many people take on more risk than they can manage in a bid to succeed. They have less experience or capacity to bear such risks. They consider it more essential to invest without knowledge than spend quality time learning and understanding the business before they venture into it. When they fail, it affects other areas of their life. They only think of gain, but they never considered that they could also fail. Everyone would love to double funds within a limited time, but it is not as easy as it seems. If you use all your money in such ventures, expecting double, when it fails, you will be in need—you will not be able to attend to the essential things.

If you see success as winning a lottery or making instant money—it could be temporary. If you lose it, you cannot get it again because it came by luck. Some even spend it all within a short time or waste it on pleasure.

It could be the situation of many people as they probably never learned to manage such resources, so they soon become poor—back to where they started.

However, if you see success as gradual growth—following the process—you learn, maintain, manage every stage, challenge and opportunity. If anything happens, you stand a better chance of knowing what to do or regaining your position. Some have spent most of their time on things that should be less important at a particular stage of their lives and ignored what should be more crucial.

A young man waited for instant money that would make him rich to buy all he wanted. He saw the possibility as his mother sought a divorce with the hope to get some amount. He did not do anything else to progress in life, just waiting. He was waiting for the process to finish, and he will become rich. He did not do anything worthwhile but mocked everyone that worked hard to progress in life. His wish came true—the divorce was successful, and he got a substantial amount from his mother. He was excited, bought a new house without a loan, furnished the house to his taste, got an automobile and some other things.

Some nine months afterwards, he ran out of money. He started begging for money to pay utility bills. He was looking for menial jobs to keep up with the bills. Instant money may be possible, but it can become a problem because of inexperience or misplaced priorities. He had his wish, but he now has more challenges than he could manage. Money, not earned, is likely to be wasted.

Some people that have nothing now think they will become rich if given one million pounds. They may need more exposure and experience to manage it. Some have had such opportunities—

they lost it all through careless spending. They spent it on what was important to them, which brought them back to where they started. The more important things were down their priority list or probably not on the list at all.

You may need a new job, so you need to devote time to search for opportunities. You will need time to prepare for interviews and make applications, but you do not have time for any of those as they are down in your list of importance. You spend time watching movies, scrolling for new clothes online, commenting on every post, religiously reading every message on all groups as soon as they come in, and probably seeking to join more every day. You will get what you use your time to do. If that is more important to you, you will get the benefit it provides, but you are unlikely to get the job you desire. It is because what it takes to get the job is far down on your priority list or probably not on it at all.

It would be worth examining your priorities to revisit the importance of everything you do and how it affects your goal. You may have been a victim of misplaced preference. You can get yourself back on track by spending more time on what is essential to achieve your goal and not what is good to do.

Chapter 25

EVALUATE YOUR DECISIONS

We make decisions—we hope they would lead us to our desired outcome. It would be great if every decision achieves that, but unfortunately, in life, it is not always the case—sometimes we make wrong decisions—the unexpected or unanticipated happens—that makes the situation worse and not better. It could also be the case in times of need.

Many people will usually come to a final decision concerning any issue based on some or many considerations. The decisions we make is a reflection of how we think and assess the situation. The difference between a good or bad decision is a function of our thoughts and considerations.

Some people may believe they have made the best decision to get help but may later discover that they were wrong. They probably misjudged, assumed or yielded to a temptation that took advantage of their needs—it is the lowest and perhaps the most vulnerable position anyone could be.

It is common for some people to neglect what they know or what is true because of their desperate need or the eagerness to get help by all means possible. The attitude makes them ignore many factors and flashing warnings that could have saved them from a wrong decision. It could be challenging for the weak-willed in times of need.

A man may decide to buy a cheap car, so cheap that it is likely to be faulty or unreliable. The man may ignore the facts and go ahead with the purchase as his best decision but later discover that he will have to pay more for repairs. The situation gets worse because he has to spend more on the car to get it to work. In a case where he cannot afford the cost of repairs, he ends up with an automobile that does not work but has gulped all the little resources he had. It is one of those situations where the cheap becomes more costly than what you thought was expensive. It could be challenging to make sound decisions in times of need, but it is crucial to evaluate them because some are not just worth it in the long run.

An entrepreneur with limited resources may use substandard goods to make his products because he cannot afford genuine parts. He may soon discover that he has not done himself or the future of his business any good. The result can only be temporary. He will likely end up in a worse position. The ability to resist that temptation is a virtue that would help build a valuable brand. Many people have attempted such fake brands or imitations—which may have attracted so many people initially, the big profits and customers began to diminish when the truth becomes revealed. The things that last may not come as quickly as we expect but usually have the characteristics of endurance and peace of mind.

It is like gathering crowds through deceit and attracting people by falsehood. It may happen, but it is usually temporary. They will leave when they discover the truth. You cannot successfully deceive all of the people all of the time. Whatever help or assistance you get through deceit will not last. The time of need could be one of the most susceptible times in the life of an individual. It implies that resisting the urge to do anything regardless of its implications is a valuable resource that can preserve the future of such individuals.

It may seem that the solution is quick, but it could eventually set one back farther than where one started. A student that is struggling with his course may consider cheating as an easy way out. It could work temporarily, but he may find himself in an unpleasant situation when caught. It is usually better to make the right decision, even if it hurts now, instead of making the wrong decision that is pleasurable now but will hurt later.

If you failed in your examination, it could be what you require to expose your weaknesses which could assist in getting the right help and assistance. It could also help reveal your strengths, gifts or abilities. The analysis of the information could lead to a better decision for your future. It is not the end, take responsibility and make better decisions.

Most often than not, the experiences we try to avoid are the experiences that could help us make the right decisions in life. If you fail a subject or endeavour, it could help you understand what you have done wrong and get help to make amends. It could also help you discover yourself or explore other things that you may be good at doing.

Some of the inventions and solutions we enjoy today came from people that made the right decisions in times of need. That is the reason why their work is still benefiting many people around the world. There may be times when you need to stop because you have failed and try something else. There could also be times you need to continue and persevere till you succeed. The decision you make is key to your success.

An American inventor and businessman, Thomas Edison, had many challenges. His teacher called him 'addled'—mentally ill—he got expelled from school. He lost his first two jobs because he was 'non-productive'. He failed one thousand times before he successfully invented the prototype of the light bulb. [1] He made some decisions despite his need that eventually made him known as America's greatest inventor.

Albert Einstein, a German-born theoretical physicist, also had a challenging experience. His parents thought he was deformed and retarded, because he could not speak until he was four, nor read till seven. His teacher called him mentally slow and expelled him from school.

At twenty-three, his father died—he had to care for his mother and sister. It was tough because he was not employed, and the family was also in significant debt. [2] He had challenging times but made decisions that eventually got him recognition as one of the greatest physicists of all time.

Henry Ford also failed several times. He could not produce a car even after using all the money from his first investors. His company suffered bankruptcy. He did not do well in politics and experienced other losses. His decisions in difficult times eventually led to what he is known for today. He founded the Ford Motor Company and played a significant role in developing the assembly line technique of mass production. [3]

Anyone that has not failed has probably not done many things. If you make mistakes, take ownership and learn from your mistakes. It will help you improve and become a better person. It will help you do better in life.

Your decision is your responsibility, but it is worth evaluating it from time to time to ensure you have the best possible outcome. The decisions you make in times of need can help change your story. I encourage you to make the best decision that will not only yield temporary benefit but long-lasting fulfilment.

THE THINGS THAT LAST MAY NOT COME
AS QUICKLY AS WE EXPECT BUT USUALLY
HAVE THE CHARACTERISTICS OF
ENDURANCE AND PEACE OF MIND.

Chapter 26

DO NOT BEG, NEGOTIATE

Most often than not, some people feel helpless because of their needs. They usually lose the sense of worth or reduce themselves to nothing— they seem to think the only way out is to be at the mercy of other people that have what they do not have. It could be challenging, but they are usually still worth more than they think if only they could understand the concept of negotiation. You will not need to beg, yet you can get more than what you need honourably—yes, without losing your sense of dignity.

You may be in a challenging situation, or it seems you have nothing left. You probably still have something, if not many, that could help you get back on track. You may get help by begging but is that the most productive? You get what people decide to give you or what they decide you need—it may include some advice or attitude that may cause you to lose the taste for any good thing they may have done. Negotiation, on the other hand, helps you get what you need based on agreement. It can help to achieve your goal, make progress in life or become independent.

Let us assume that a man has lost his job and needs money. He also thinks he has nothing of value. A friend found that he could produce bread and confectioneries. He also has a lot of customers that like his bread and confectioneries. His excuse for begging is that he has lost his job, he has nothing left—He needs money. When told about the idea of baking, he has excuses—he does not have money to start the business, no commercial baking equipment, no money to buy raw materials. 'I need money for everything.'

Some people get stuck in a similar position today and never see a way to progress because they do not have what they need. You may have discovered that someone has it, and you can also have it for your use to achieve your own goal by negotiation. Yes, you do not have everything you require, but you can negotiate to get what you do not have from those that have it. You may not even need to pay for it from your pocket if you make favourable arrangements.

Let us consider what the man in the example above could do without money. He has skill and customers but nothing to produce. What does he need to get the income? Raw materials, commercial baking equipment, and so on. He could negotiate to get those things, producing a business plan to share the risks and profits. Every party contributes to the business, shares the risks and profits in proportion according to their negotiation. If it is a convincing deal, they will part with their resources to contribute to the idea. The man will have some gain that he would be proud of, and every party that contributed will also be a beneficiary when the idea succeeds. It could also fail, but every party shares the failure as well. It is an opportunity, if well harnessed, that could help initiate a change of circumstance.

Some professionals or traders have fallen victim to hard times, but they still have their skills and a track record of good performance. They do not have money to buy raw materials or goods to sell. They could negotiate with those that have it and come up with an agreement that benefits those involved. They receive the raw materials and process them to finished products, using their skills, time and energy. The sale of the products brings benefits to everyone that contributed. It could be an effective way to get back on track with low risk.

You can negotiate your way out of need. There could be services that could help you depending on what you have and what you need. I know of some organisations that set up solutions that give access to people that require professional services. They help you produce your product at no cost to you. They sell it and share the profit according to the negotiated agreement and pay you your share. It is a win-win situation. You may not make as much profit as if you provided everything yourself, but you would not have made anything without them because you did not have everything you needed in the first place.

A young man once approached my car as I parked at a car park. He was hungry and would like to eat, but he did not beg for money. He offered to wash my car so that I could pay him for the service. I thought it was an honourable approach, although I gave him more than he could have gotten and told him he did not need to wash my car.

There could be some opportunities to earn money with dignity, which could help you get back on track. You could probably offer services to your neighbour, friends and colleagues. You do not have a job—you are available all day and need money. You can help other people with their needs or relevant services they pay for or would be willing to pay you for doing it. It is about offering value and helping them. If you could use your time to add value to others or make life easy or convenient, they could be willing to pay for your time. It could be anything you can do like to pick up groceries from a shop, house chores, cooking, gardening, fixing faulty equipment, school runs, installing new machines, among others. They could be some ways to earn some money.

I know of a young man that helps with the assembly of furniture in his local area. He uses his time and energy productively. Many women benefit from his service and give good food and money for his services. He is happy to get his need met while he meets the needs of others—it is a win-win situation.

If you have something you are good at doing, you can offer it to others. Look for those that need what you have, offer it at competitive prices, and you would be surprised that you have been wasting time all along. You can teach, but you do not have a job yet? Some students local to you could benefit from your skill. You can drive, but you are doing nothing at the moment? It can earn you some income. You may find someone with a car they do not use, or probably someone with a car but cannot drive. A good agreement can give you what you need and will benefit the parties involved. Waiting to get all you need may not be wise because you can use what you have now to negotiate to get what you need.

You can start something small with low risk. You can commence a business by engaging friends and family to help and share the risks and profits. Encourage everyone involved to learn to do what is involved, and you would see the business grow. It may not be perfect, but it could help you identify abilities that could change your situation. The feedback could help you believe in it and provide the confidence to do more. A young man once got his siblings to contribute time, energy or any available resource to an idea. It was low risk as they had little or nothing to lose because they did not engage their time in any other productive thing. If they succeeded, however, it would change their situation for the better.

You may be in need, but you have access to some raw materials, someone has machinery that could process the raw materials, someone else has space for processing, and someone else has potential buyers for the end product. You cannot produce and finish the end product to make the maximum profit from those raw materials. You can negotiate and collaborate with everyone that could help you along the way by sharing the profit and challenges. You will get more profit and experience than waiting for a sudden change of circumstance.

It may be a good idea to think of what you have and consider how you can use them to get what you need on your way to where you desire to be in the future. You may be worth more than you think if you consider negotiating for what you do not have.

YOU CAN NEGOTIATE YOUR WAY OUT OF NEED.

Chapter 27

WHY HELP FAILS?

One of the most frustrating news to hear in times of need is probably one that announces that the help you have trusted so much is not forthcoming. Have you ever wondered why some people could help you in the past but under what seems to be a similar situation, they could not at a different time?

Have you been there, in a situation you felt so confident that someone will help you because he has done so in the past, but to your surprise, you got the news you never expected, you got the shock you never anticipated—it did not work on this occasion. Why would help fail?

Many years ago, a man took his car to his mechanic for repairs just like he would always do.

He anticipated a quick fix because his mechanic has a track record of timely and excellent service. He expected to get his car back in a matter of a few hours to have it ready for the busy week he has ahead of him. It has always worked—the mechanic always surpasses his expectations, so there were enough reasons to think the same way, but he was wrong in this particular situation.

The mechanic identified the problem, he could fix it, but he needed to replace some faulty parts in the car. The big problem is that some of those parts were not available anywhere locally. It had to be requested and ordered from abroad. It could take weeks or months depending on the availability of the product and the time it takes to arrive, among others factors.

The mechanic could not get his car back in minutes or few hours as he used to, so the man was frustrated because he has always thought the man could help in the same way, with anything relating to the car. Some people think the same way and may not understand the limitations of those that offer to help.

Why was the mechanic unable to deliver as he did previously? Why is he unable to help even though he has helped many times in the past? I discovered that the help the mechanic could render depends on the availability of spare parts, among other things. The reason he could help so quickly was that there were spare parts readily available to him. It implies that he becomes helpless when he does not have access to the required spare parts.

It explains the frustration or dilemma of many people today. They never realised that the help they received is not only dependent on the person helping them. It is also a function of some other factors that make it possible for the person to help on which he also depends. You may never have had the opportunity to know it, but those that have experienced it are likely to understand the implications of dependence on others that in turn, depend on others for help.

The mechanic indeed has some skills and expertise which are required. However, it becomes irrelevant because he cannot progress with the work without the spare parts. He could only be of help to the man when the spare parts are available. When support fails, most often than not, it is dependent on something outside of the control of those willing to help.

The reason the mechanic could not help was that his help depends on the spare part. The reason the local spare parts stores could not help is that they rely on distributors. The distributors also depend on the manufacturers to produce them. It is a chain of events that eventually affected the failure of help to the car owner.

A lawyer relies on the law to help fight for justice. If the law does not support justice, the lawyer does not have anything with which to help. The skill depends on the law—when the law is absent, it will not benefit people facing trials. There are many victims of injustice today in many places, not because there are no lawyers but no law to support justice.

The dentist depends on proven medication for patients. When you visit the dentist with unbearable pain in your teeth, the specialist recommends some medication after examining the symptoms. The help provided is only possible because he could recognise the signs. He also knows the prescription or process that could solve the problem. The medication is also made available by a manufacturer, distributed to a pharmacy and dispensed by a local pharmacist. If the expert cannot ascertain the reason for your pain or identify any known medication or find any in production, he would not help your situation. Your pain will continue even though you have visited a specialist dentist. The help you get depends on many other things, not just the dentist—if missing, it fails.

A group of firefighters could fail in stopping a fire or saving lives. Yes, if they do not have the required equipment, like a ladder long enough or the required extinguisher. The help they could offer depends on something outside of them, the absence of which makes the venture a failure. There are occasions where the experts watch helplessly while the fire ravages properties or lives, not because they do not want to help, but their help depends on something else to succeed.

A group of pilots could helplessly watch a plane crash because they are dependent on the controls in the aircraft. If they do not work as expected, the team of pilots become helpless. Their skills can only manage the plane using the control buttons. That is why we have seen many crashes despite the skills and expertise of the crew on board.

It is not just the skilled pilots—yes, they are required, but everything they depend upon to help must also be in good working order.

Have you felt frustrated because the support you so desired did not work as planned? You may have thought someone failed to help you, but it may not be in their hands even though they may have helped in the past. It may be something outside of their control which they also depend on to help.

Chapter 28

TRACE THE SOURCE

Have you bought a product and needed help because something has gone wrong? Are you frustrated because of a piece of expensive equipment you got that does not work as expected? Is your business at a standstill because you purchased a machine that cannot produce as you anticipated? Are you incurring losses because the machinery your business relies upon is malfunctioning? It is usually frustrating. It could be more frustrating when you go around seeking help, but no one seems to know what to do—they could damage it or make it worse.

As you may have noticed, every product has a name and a manufacturer. They usually include their details as part of the product. The documents contain the recommended guide to help should anything happen to the product. It also provides information on how to use it and what to do when you notice some symptoms.

A man once took his electronic device to a local repair shop for repairs. He was surprised to hear what the technician had to say after checking it. He said: Sorry, I cannot help you. The man was confused and wanted to know more. Are you busy? If that is the case, I do not mind waiting. Is it costly to fix? I would not mind the cost. Is it going to take a long time to resolve? I would not mind, he said, seeking to know the reason. He replied, no, not any of those. I have no training to enable me to work on this device. You need to contact the manufacturer for help. They would probably fix it for free or give you another one if it is still under warranty.

The man then remembered he had those details when he got the device. He contacted the manufacturer and got directed to an authorised dealer close to him that could help him. It got fixed at no extra cost to him. There was help available that he never thought was there.

Sometimes in life, we look for help only in familiar places. It works sometimes, but unfortunately, they may not always be the best places. You can trace the product back to its source, and you could discover that you have genuine assistance waiting for you. It may be the company that sold it to you or the organisation that made the product if they differ, but what you need may only be a phone call away. You may have access to the manufacturer's help that will not cost you any extra, but probably you do not know.

You probably bought a product that did not work, or it is the wrong one. You could get help and assistance. There could be provisions to return the item within a limited period to get your money back or choose another. It is common for manufacturers to offer a guarantee for their products. They are willing to accept a return if you have reasons to return it within a reasonable period. The product may have a known fault—which is of no error of your own—that you got to know after purchase. The manufacturer could help with such, which makes you free from any unplanned expenses.

A landlord spent so much on the renovation of his property. Some time afterwards, he began to notice some unpleasant signs that made him worried. He was upset as he was scared of the cost to fix it again. He was wise enough to tell someone that gave him some advice and asked some questions: Who did it for you? Who made the products? Which companies were involved? The answers led to the help he required. The contractors that did the work got in touch with the companies that supplied the products—they also got in touch with the manufacturers. The good news is that the repair work got completed at no extra cost to the landlord. It was a happy ending and a great relief—it may not be the case if he did not trace the source.

Many years ago, a young student bought a motorcycle in a village—where he stayed for a temporary assignment—but did not register it as it was not a legal requirement there. He later relocated to the city and took it with him. He found that he could not use it except it was registered. An attempt to get it recorded brought about suspicion as it was no longer new and never had a legal record. It was strange but true, although difficult to prove to those in the city. He decided to contact the store that sold it to him in the village, and they were willing to help complete all the necessary documentation for the registration. He got the help he needed by tracing the source.

An employee once visited a store to purchase some items using a voucher he got from his company. The cashier rejected it as it was not familiar. The employee insisted that it should be checked and verified. The managers on duty were able to confirm that it was acceptable and genuine. He got the help that saved him from the embarrassment.

If you know where a product came from, you are likely to get from there information that would prove helpful in resolving the problem you may be experiencing. You may find that the help you need could be in agreements, contracts, and other forms of documentation exchanged in business transactions. Many people never attempt to read them but assume they could always figure out what to do when the problem arises.

There was once a passenger on a ship who refused to eat any food or drink anything served. He was hungry and desired the food he saw—it was hard to resist the aroma, but throughout the journey, he said no. He had a valid ticket, and he was entitled to every meal as a result, but he did not check from the source to confirm. He assumed he had to pay for it. He decided to live on crackers and water that he brought with him. Someone that got worried just before they got to the destination asked him why he refused to eat. He responded that he did not have money, but the co-passenger then enlightened him that the food and drinks were all part of the ticket. If only he had checked from the source, he would have had the confidence to position himself for a sumptuous meal.

You may be frustrated because you think there is no help for you. It may not be the case—you may only have been seeking help where there is none.

Chapter 29

CONNECT TO SOURCE

You may have enjoyed the benefits of some products but never knew those that made them. You may have benefited from services that have helped fix problems relating to some products but never considered the need to know the manufacturer. I have found that it is true in many cases that many enjoy products and never get to know where they came from or who made them.

A man bought a car many years ago from a car dealer. He was excited to have it, but he never met the manufacturer. He got documents that provided information about the manufacturer stating that the new buyer should fill those forms and send them back to the manufacturer. He ignored the request, kept the documents, never sent it back as requested by the manufacturer. He said that he knows it is a good product, which fulfils the purpose for which he bought it and represented good value for money. I do not need any forms; I do not need the manufacturer—I know what to do.

The car developed some fault some years later, and he decided to go to his favourite mechanic for assistance. The mechanic contacted the manufacturer for guidance on the issue and how to get the spare parts to replace any faulty ones. The mechanic got what he wanted and solved the problem—the car was back on the road again. Do you know why he could fix the car? I wonder what you think. The mechanic was able to help because the manufacturer provided information and produced parts for the benefit of all. If the manufacturers did not make parts for their cars, his effort would have yielded no result.

The car owner went away excited because he got his car fixed by the mechanic. He praises him for such great work. He did not realise that he could help him only because he contacted the manufacturer for parts and instructions. The car owner probably drove away confident that he does not need the manufacturer after all.

I wonder, are you like that man that ignores manuals, disregards information and request to connect to the manufacturer? Many people do not know the manufacturer of the products they use. The fact that the products work as they should without the visibility of those that made it may make them disregard or even claim ignorance of their existence. Moreover, they can access assistance because the manufacturers have provided guides, parts, and information to many others that could help fix the problems they have with their products.

There are so many choices when seeking assistance—they all seem to provide support. However, not all are approved or recommended by the manufacturer. They usually insist on taking their products to those that have gotten their approval. You may also have observed that some others may attempt to fix it, even though they are not recommended—the experiences are not usually the same as some have ended up with unpleasant surprises.

I remember another man that bought a car from a car dealer. He registered the car and used it as recommended, following all the guidelines. A few years afterwards, the manufacturer predicted a fault in the particular brand. It made them send letters to all those that bought that model. There was a recall because of a potential safety issue. He got the letter stating that they anticipate some faults in the model that could cause problems and would like him to return the car as soon as possible for a free check-up and fix. The manufacturer wrote him because he was registered and known to the source. They know the details of those that have registered as owners of their products.

Manufacturers do not only produce parts, guides and training, but they are also interested in a continuous relationship with those that use their products. They provide forms to register so they can connect with them. It helps to provide regular updates, which may include assistance whenever they foresee a problem.

Your computer has an operating system and some other software that run on it to perform different functions. They are products that get regular updates, patches and fixes when connected to the manufacturer. The products work because the manufacturers keep working to provide support to help the product perform its functions.

A medical doctor can attend to a patient because he has learnt about diseases from consistent evidence and can apply the knowledge. The reason he could prescribe medication is that scientists have proven through consistent trials that it can work. The pharmaceutical companies can produce it because there are materials available in nature proven to have the required ingredients.

The doctor cannot help if he does not know the diseases, or the medication is unknown or unavailable, or the raw material for production is not available in nature. His help will fail not because he is unqualified or does not want to assist—but because he depends on something else to make his assistance a success.

We are all products of The Creator. He provides all that we need through different sources and different people. He gives rain and sunshine to all regardless of their belief, nationality, age, or ethnicity. We can see his works in nature. He is the manufacturer that many have ignored—The God that many refuse to acknowledge. They never thought that the assistance they receive was from Him.

You are one of those products, and your creator would like to connect with you. If you can trace the source of the help you enjoy, you will discover that there is a great God behind it all. Many have not acknowledged it, and others have not connected, but that does not mean He does not exist. If you agree or disagree, that does not change anything. The manufacturers keep producing parts, offering training and support for their products even when those that use them fail to acknowledge it. Likewise, The God of all creation keeps providing help and support for all, including you.

I will encourage you to seek Him with all your heart. Find Him and connect to the source of all help.

Chapter 30

CHOOSE TO RECOVER

Many things limit what you can or cannot do. The challenges you face in life are attempts to hinder your ability. As you discover how to find help and navigate through the challenging phases of your life, you have more hope to face the future. You can learn to scale through those barriers that once held you down.

You could be a better person if you know how to handle the limitation in your life. You would perhaps be able to do more if you knew how to overcome the difficulties that you face. Life could be less stressful if you know better ways of doing what you are doing. You could enjoy more fulfilment and progress if you know how to get the help you need.

The more you know, the better you live. The more knowledge you have, the better your approach towards the problems that come your way—the more victories you have.

As you find answers, you are also equipping yourself to help other people. You have the confidence to help others when you have gained freedom from the same challenge in the past.

You can also help others to live by adding value to them. They also would find the solution to their needs and then also add value to others.

There are three categories of people that you could interact with as you journey in life.

The first are those people that have what you need. These are the people that would help you or has helped you. They provide the education, support, or encouragement you need to overcome your challenges. You will go to them, or they come to you to provide such assistance. You can benefit from the people in this category in various ways. You can always find what works best for you in your current circumstance.

The second group are those the need what you have. These are people going through the same challenges you have just gone through or those about to go through the same or similar experience. Your experiences will be of help to them. They may come to you, or you go them, but they would benefit from your transformation. You can create avenues to help and meet those needs.

The third are those that have what you have and need what you need. These are in the same stage or level as you, and you have the opportunity to grow together and collaborate to become better and achieve more. You can do more with more people having the same focus and attacking the same problem.

Your life can benefit from the help of others to make you a better person. Others can benefit from you to make them better people. You can work with others to make many more people better people.

Make the right decisions and take the appropriate steps from where you are to where you desire to be.

The power to choose is in your hands; do something about your situation. You have what it takes; take what you have and decide to make a difference.

You can recover, and when you do, help others also.

YOU COULD ENJOY MORE FULFILMENT
AND PROGRESS IF YOU KNOW HOW TO GET
THE HELP YOU NEED.

REFERENCES

Chapter 1: It Is Not Bizarre

[1] The Economist, "Virgin Looks for Help," *The Economist*, Jun. 11, 2020.
https://www.economist.com/business/2020/06/11/virgin-looks-for-help (accessed Aug. 14, 2021)..

[2] The Guardian, "Virgin Atlantic to Seek Millions in State Aid amid Covid-19 Slump," *The Guardian*, Mar. 27, 2020.
https://www.theguardian.com/business/2020/mar/27/virgin-atlantic-to-seek-millions-in-state-aid-amid-covid-19-slump (accessed Aug. 14, 2021).

Chapter 6: Help Is near, I Never Knew

[1] The Incredible Journey, "Meet Your Marvellous

Brain - The Incredible Journey,"
www.youtube.com, Aug. 10, 2018.
https://www.youtube.com/watch?v=ycSSChCt0_o
(accessed Aug. 16, 2021).

Chapter 10: The Virtues of Tenacity

[1] Old Farmer's Almanac, "Tomatoes," *Old Farmer's Almanac*, May 19, 2019.
https://www.almanac.com/plant/tomatoes
(accessed Aug. 16, 2021).

[2] StarK Bros, "Berry Plants: How Many Years until Fruit?," *Stark Bro's Nurseries & Orchards Co.*
https://www.starkbros.com/growing-guide/article/how-many-years-berries (accessed Aug. 16, 2021).

[3] S. Albert, "How to Grow Apples - Harvest to Table," *Harvest to Table*, Jul. 26, 2009.
https://harvesttotable.com/how_to_grow_apples / (accessed Aug. 16, 2021).

Chapter 13: Learn from the past

[1] Statista, "Taiwan: Novel Coronavirus Development 2021," *Statista.* https://www.statista.com/statistics/1108537/taiwan-novel-coronavirus-covid19-confirmed-death-recovered-trend/ (accessed Aug. 18, 2021).

[2]C. Farr and M. Gao, "How Taiwan Beat the Coronavirus," *CNBC*, Jul. 15, 2020. https://www.cnbc.com/2020/07/15/how-taiwan-beat-the-coronavirus.html (accessed Aug. 18, 2021).

[3]Y. Tan, "Covid-19: What Went Wrong in Singapore and Taiwan?," *BBC News*, May 19, 2021.

Chapter 16: All I Need Is Help

[1] BBC, "Puberty Blocker Ruling 'protects Vulnerable teens,'" *BBC News*, Dec. 01, 2020.

[2]Tat Bellamy-Walker, "Instead of Arresting a

Woman Accused of shoplifting, These NYPD Officers Paid for Her Meal," *CNN*, Jul. 05, 2019. https://edition.cnn.com/2019/07/05/us/nypd-officers-whole-foods-trnd/index.html (accessed Aug. 23, 2021).

Chapter 18: You Are in School

[1]B. Artz, A. Goodall, and A. J. Oswald, "If Your Boss Could Do Your Job, You're More Likely to Be Happy at Work," *Harvard Business Review*, Dec. 29, 2016. https://hbr.org/2016/12/if-your-boss-could-do-your-job-youre-more-likely-to-be-happy-at-work (accessed Aug. 23, 2021).

Chapter 25: Evaluate Your Decisions

[1]T. Hasker, "How Thomas Edison's Mother Was the Making of Him...," *Legends Report*, May 24, 2020. https://www.legends.report/how-thomas-edisons-mother-was-the-making-of-him/ (accessed Aug. 27, 2021).

[2]Business Insider, "Albert Einstein's Childhood Nickname Was 'the Dopey one,'" *TheJournal.ie*, Oct. 24, 2015. https://www.thejournal.ie/life-of-albert-einstein-2406681-Oct2015/ (accessed Aug. 27, 2021).

[3]Year On, "Overcoming Failure: the Perseverance of Henry Ford*,"* *Yearon.com*, Dec. 06, 2014. https://www.yearon.com/blog/successes-of-henry-ford (accessed Aug. 27, 2021).

Thank you

Thank you for investing in this book. I hope you enjoyed reading it as much as it has been a pleasure for me to write it, and I trust that it has helped you.

It would be helpful to me and many others if you could share your experience by way of a review or a comment.

Please write to:

iph@TheServantandKing.com

We would be glad to hear from you.

Looking for more?

Please visit:

www.TheServantandKing.com

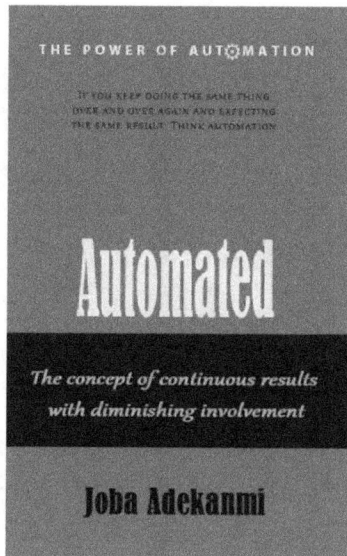

THE POWER OF AUT⊛MATION

IF YOU KEEP DOING THE SAME THING
OVER AND OVER AGAIN AND EXPECTING
THE SAME RESULT: THINK AUTOMATION

Automated

*The concept of continuous results
with diminishing involvement*

Joba Adekanmi

Automated: The concept of continuous results with diminishing involvement.

IF YOU KEEP DOING THE SAME THING
OVER AND OVER AGAIN AND EXPECTING
THE SAME RESULT: THINK AUTOMATION.

Let this book inspire you to productivity!

Available on Amazon or your local bookstore.

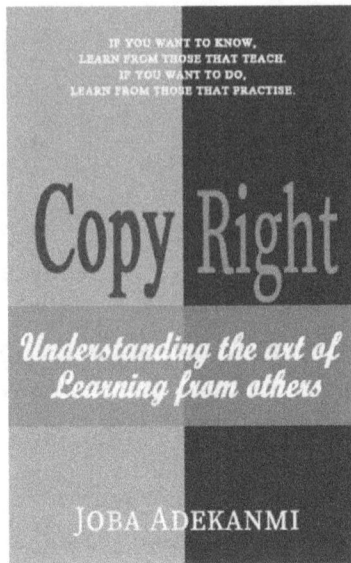

Copy Right:
Understanding the Art of Learning from Others.

IF YOU WANT TO KNOW,
LEARN FROM THOSE THAT TEACH.
IF YOU WANT TO DO,
LEARN FROM THOSE THAT PRACTISE.

This book, with permeating shrewdness and practical stories, exposes the influence of other people. It will help you understand the impact on your life.

Available on Amazon or your local bookstore.

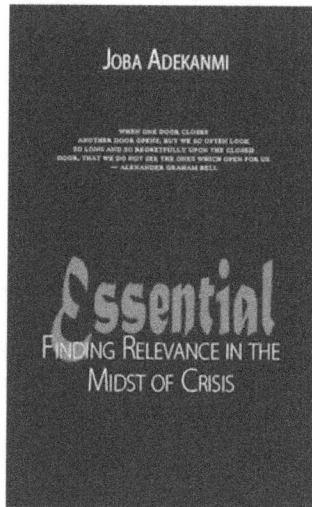

JOBA ADEKANMI

WHEN ONE DOOR CLOSES
ANOTHER DOOR OPENS, BUT WE SO OFTEN LOOK
SO LONG AND SO REGRETFULLY UPON THE CLOSED
DOOR, THAT WE DO NOT SEE THE ONES WHICH OPEN FOR US
— ALEXANDER GRAHAM BELL

Essential FINDING RELEVANCE IN THE MIDST OF CRISIS

Essential: Finding Relevance in the Midst of Crisis

WHEN ONE DOOR CLOSES
ANOTHER DOOR OPENS; BUT WE SO OFTEN LOOK
SO LONG AND SO REGRETFULLY UPON THE CLOSED
DOOR, THAT WE DO NOT SEE THE ONES WHICH OPEN FOR US.
— ALEXANDER GRAHAM BELL

In Essential, you will find some clear and actionable advice that will help to restore hope and encourage you to step out and make the most of any situation. You are essential because you can make yourself relevant even when things change.

Available on Amazon or your local bookstore.

www.ingramcontent.com/pod-product-compliance
Lightning Source LLC
LaVergne TN
LVHW051231080426
835513LV00016B/1523